"A brilliant concept and a wonderful read, *Conscious Entrepreneurs* catapults its readers into a refreshing new paradigm of true service, soul gratification and win/win empowerment. A new dawn of Conscious Entrepreneurs has clearly begun."

~ARIOLE K. ALEI, Author of *H.O.P.E. = Healing Ourselves and Planet Earth*
www.heartsongsolutions.ca

"This book is a beautiful catalyst that will help you to Learn, Grow and Expand your life into what you would LOVE it to be. Well worth reading."

~ GARY STEELE, Author of *Open Your Heart Firefly*

"*Conscious Entrepreneurs* brings to together an eclectic and wise group of entrepreneurs who share the single trait of their incredible consciousness and the lessons they have learned in building their successful businesses. The wisdom here is not to be missed if you want to expand your business and do it with ease, freedom and conscious design!"

~ JACKIE LAPIN, Bestselling Author of *The Art of Conscious Creation,*
How You Can Transform the World

"*Conscious Entrepreneurs,* is a refreshing approach to achieving a life filled with purpose, passion and profit. Christine Kloser has brought together an incredible group of entrepreneurs who show through their own example that creating a joyful, abundant, successful and spiritual life is as close as ones thoughts, beliefs and vision. I would recommend this book to anyone who is ready to embrace all the gifts awaiting you."

~ Dr. Joe Capista, Author of *What Can a Dentist Teach*
You About Business, Life and Success!

"An enlightening way to look at entrepreneurship. *Conscious Entrepreneurs* puts a new and vital spin on what it takes to be successful in this exciting, yet demanding approach to business ownership."

~ CHRIS FINLEY, Chief Operating Officer, SurveyMonkey.com

"The most important component of business…is people! Not money! Conscious Entrepreneurs helps entrepreneurs and business leaders proactively and creatively re-think, re-structure and re-design who they are in their business…and how they run their business so that it works for them! This is an amazing business handbook to be read…and re-read!"

~ JIM HORAN, Author/creator of *The One Page Business Plan* book series

"Christine Kloser has done it again. In yet another masterfully crafted book on abundance and prosperity, *Conscious Entrepreneurs* is one you'll want to add to your own personal success library as well as give to your friends, colleagues and associates. With example after example from successful entrepreneurs who have walked the walk, *Conscious Entrepreneurs* shows you how truly simple creating a life of success, happiness, joy and abundance can actually be."

~ KATHLEEN GAGE, Author, Speaker, Mentor

"Are you really ready to engage our evolving economy? Read *Conscious Entrepreneurs!* It provides holistic business strategies that transform the consciousness in commerce!"

~ BRANDON LONDON D. KLAYMAN, Owner of Conscious Commerce

"*Conscious Entrepreneurs* is a fresh approach to being successful in owning a business. Offering both practical advice and inspirational insight, every entrepreneur should keep a copy of this unique book on hand."

~ CB SCHOTTLAND, President – Paragon Innovations Group, LLC

"An inspiring and passionate approach to experiencing entrepreneurial success and fulfillment."

~VANESSA SUMMERS, named 'Financial Guru' by *CNBC*
Author of *The Girl's Guide to Money & Investing* and *Buying Solo*

"Conscious Entrepreneurs are revolutionaries blazing a trail to lives of prosperity and alignment with your soul's purpose. This inspiring book shares beautifully how you can create a way so that your professional success doesn't come at the expense of your personal happiness. A definite must read book!"

~ CAROLYN ELLIS, Founder of ThriveAfterDivorce.com
and Author of *The 7 Pitfalls of Single Parenting*

"As an entrepreneur who is all too familiar with the road less traveled, this is the book I wish I had when I started on my journey."

~BETH DAVIS, CEO of HandAnalyst.com and
2007-2008 Glazer-Kennedy Information Marketer of the Year

"You'll resonate with this wonderful collection of advice from successful authors and business leaders. Christine has done it again with providing insight on how conscious entrepreneurship can help you live your work life with purpose!"

~ CHARLENE M. PROCTOR, PH.D. Best selling author of *Let Your Goddess Grow!* and *The Women's Book of Empowerment*

"Heart, Compassion, Longing for Service, all driving forces that form the heart and soul of *Conscious Entrepreneurs*. You'll immediately feel connected, supported, uplifted, and surrounded by the unique energies and qualities offered in this radical recipe for enjoying a passionate, purposeful and profitable business. Invite the wisdom and generosity to guide you into your greater birthright by saying 'Yes!' to your bigger 'why.' You won't be able to go about 'business as usual' and the world will forever rejoice your decision!"

~ ANITA PATHIK LAW, Author of *The Power of Our Way;
A Path to a Collective Consciousness and Awakening the Healer Within*

"*Conscious Entrepreneurs* is a brilliant collection of insights and strategies from new thought leaders for the spiritually minded entrepreneurs who ask the question, 'How can I create a wildly successful soul-based business and have a fulfilling life?' A must-read for anyone ready to take the leap from surviving to thriving!"
~ LORRAINE COHEN, CEO Powerfull Living, Coach, Speaker and Broadcaster

"What a powerful book. It explores so well what the truly conscious entrepreneur knows; that business growth and development is impossible to separate from personal growth and development. If you desire to really make a difference in the world, as well as make money in business, then this book is an invaluable resource for you."
~ JANET BECKERS, Founder of Wonderful Web Women

"A new awakening for all of those who want to answer a calling to create a business based on your personal gifts. *Conscious Entrepreneurs* is just the blueprint to realizing your gift"
~ BRETT JOHNSON, Owner, Main Street Design Company

"*Conscious Entrepreneurs* is an essential guide for every entrepreneur searching for fresh ideas and a deeper purpose in business and in life."
~ DR. LIN MOREL, Internationally renowned speaker, author, and CEO of the Beyond Words Group, Inc.

"*Conscious Entrepreneurs* is a model for living your life and growing your business intuitively- I love this book!"
~ SUZEE EBELING PCC, President, Center for Intuitive Learning

"This book is a great idea. In your hands you hold the key to enjoying your profit with purpose."
~ JOHN CASTAGNINI, Creator of Thank God I...

"*Conscious Entrepreneurs* is an inspiring collection of wisdom and advice from the trailblazers who have chosen the path of freedom, fulfillment and purpose."
~ GINNY WILLIAMS, Professional Business and Life Coach

"From beginning the entrepreneurial journey to thriving in your ultimate business, Christine Kloser's brilliant compilation, *Conscious Entrepreneurs*, illuminates the path for those of us who long, not merely to create a successful business, but to answer our true spiritual calling. A heartfelt and richly inspiring guidebook, *Conscious Entrepreneurs* is destined to become a new business classic."
~ ELLEN BRITT, PA, ED.D. Co-founder - EveryDayQi.com

CONSCIOUS
ENTREPRENEURS

A Radical New Approach
to Purpose, Passion & Profit

[signature]

Love Your Life

Love Your Life Publishing
Dallastown, PA

(page 71)

Published by:
Love Your Life Publishing
PO Box 2, Dallastown, PA 17313
www.LoveYourLifeBooks.com

ISBN: 978-0-9798554-7-4
Library of Congress Control No: 2008904802

Cover design, layout and typesetting by Cyanotype Book Architects
Editing by Marlene Oulton, Write Choice Virtual Assistants
Author Photo by Joe Henson, New York, NY

Printed in the United States of America

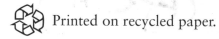 Printed on recycled paper.

A portion of the proceeds from the sale of this book will be donated to Trees for the Future (www.treesftf.org).

To those entrepreneurs who hear the call
to make a difference in the world.

Table of Contents

PART II: LIVING YOUR FULL POTENTIAL

Introduction

Thank you for picking up this book and reading it! Whether you have dreams of becoming an entrepreneur, or are already pursuing your entrepreneurial dreams, this book offers radical new insights on how to blend your purpose and passion with profit.

Why *Conscious Entrepreneurs*? *Conscious Entrepreneurs* is about **shining light** on the conscious business MOVEMENT; giving it a **name,** giving it **power** and giving a strong **voice to the pioneers** who are leading the way for millions more to come. The fact that you are reading this right now is assurance that you, too, are part of this movement; for which I am grateful.

You see, I believe what Neale Donald Walsch, author of *Conversations with God,* said in the foreword to my book *The Freedom Formula: How to Put Soul in Your Business and Money in Your Bank.* He said:

"Business is your highest spiritual understanding, demonstrated."

I resonated with his words so deeply that **when I first heard them I started to cry.** It was then that I knew... I had to publish a book about conscious business. It felt as if I was being called to take a stand for this new way of conducting business as an entrepreneur.

But, I wanted to do more than publish my own book. I wanted to also **give voice to many entrepreneurs who were hearing the same call.** Collectively, we have a **much greater impact** than any one of our voices alone.

My company, Love Your Life Publishing, has helped nearly three hundred entrepreneurs become published authors (the majority of those in anthologies similar to this). In my four years of publishing and working with hundreds of entrepreneurs, I was completely astonished at the record speed in which the chapters of this book were filled. I had never had such a response to any "call for submissions" as I did for this book. Not only did the forty-seven chapters fill up in record time, but I had a waiting list with dozens more authors who I sadly, just didn't have room for in this volume. I share this success with you because it is PROOF of the growing number of entrepreneurs being called to this new way of conducting business.

For me personally, this book is about **leaving a legacy of a better world...** for my daughter, the children in your family, and ALL families for generations to come. We live in such critical times right now; times filled with the **amazing potential to usher in a more peaceful, harmonious, and conscious way of life.** I believe that raising awareness of a new way of doing business is an essential piece for seeing the shifts we all hope for.

It has been an honor and a thrill to bring this book to life, and I am grateful for the forty-seven like-minded entrepreneurs who share their personal stories, strategies and successes here with you. You wouldn't be holding this book in your hands if it weren't for them all saying "yes" to their call.

Here's to conscious entrepreneurs changing the world!

To your freedom,

Christine

Christine Kloser
Compiler/Publisher, *Conscious Entrepreneurs*

PART I:

Your Journey of Success

CHAPTER 1

Your Playing Small Does Not Serve the World

Dawn Z. Bournand

"The greatest danger for most of us is not that our aim is too high and we miss it, but that it is too low and we reach it."

~ MICHELANGELO

So you have decided to take the leap and follow your dream of becoming an entrepreneur. Congratulations! Now, let me ask you something, have you made the decision to be hugely successful? If you respond with a resounding yes, good for you, but, if you answered no, why haven't you? If you are serious about becoming a conscious entrepreneur and making a real difference, you need to plan to succeed and the larger your success, the larger the contribution you can make.

If you need a bit of convincing, here are seven reasons why your playing small does not serve the world and why growing both yourself and your business to a naturally abundant state will help you best give back.

Realizing your full potential is your purpose here.

You are meant to stretch, to change and to grow. If you ever doubt this, look to nature for its example of constant renewal and growth. Since you too, are governed by the laws of nature, it is only logical that you will go through your own renewal and growth.

"Men are born to succeed, not to fail."

– HENRY DAVID THOREAU

When you plant yourself in a healthy environment and surround yourself with positive influences and inputs, you will naturally grow to the full potential that you have within yourself. Perhaps in the past, you may have settled for just getting by or at best being comfortable. What you may not realize is that your optimum potential can only be achieved when you immerse yourself in the optimum environment.

Be aware that even if you are in positive surroundings, you will still have to take steps to make things happen. Are you constantly working towards your goals, or are you waiting for just the right moment? What if you really could begin to live the life that you know you were destined to lead right now? You can! Simply decide that there is no better time than the present and take that first step.

When you are working towards your highest potential, you inspire others and pave paths for them to follow as well.

People love role models. We all want heroes and heroines. Not to mention, it is simply more comfortable to take a path that has already been proven. Finding someone to model yourself and your path to success after is not only smart it is infinitely easier.

"I am looking for a lot of men who have an infinite capacity to not know what can't be done."

~ HENRY FORD

When you have a mentor to help you in your quest for success, the learning process becomes a pleasure. They can show you things to avoid and shortcuts to take, and may also help you make valuable acquaintances that will advance your business infinitely quicker than when trying to do it all alone.

Growing yourself and your business takes courage, but through your daring and your risk taking, you will motivate others. They will see that if you can do it, perhaps they can too. Use your position at the top to pull others up with you.

There is nothing noble in being broke.

Even today the stereotype that a truly spiritual man is one who gives all his worldly possessions away to others and holds on to nothing for himself still prevails. This twisted logic makes no sense whatsoever, especially when you realize that those who can give mountains of money are those who have it.

"It is one of the beautiful compensations of this life that no man can sincerely try to help another without helping himself."

~ RALPH WALDO EMERSON

Money is a form of energy, and when used in the right way can help thousands, even hundreds of thousands. Give yourself permission right now to become a raging financial success. Through a thriving business you will be able to give whenever you see a worthy cause or someone in need, what could be more noble and gratifying than that? The opportunities are unlimited, the good that can be done is thrilling, and money is the motor to make it all happen. Begin to welcome the thought of having money and release all of the negative stories you have been creating around this incredible source of energy.

People who resent your success are not the people you want in your life under any circumstances.

A true friend wants your highest good, your ultimate fulfillment and your upmost happiness. Choose to surround yourself with those who help you reach higher and broader.

"If you want to fly with eagles, don't swim with ducks! I make it a point to only associate with successful, positive people and just as importantly, I disassociate from negative ones."

~ T. HARV EKER

Surround yourself with like minded people, and form a support system to venture out into the unknown. Choose wisely and find people who will help you test your limits. Not only were you meant to fly, you were meant to soar - to reach heights you never dreamed possible. If you ever feel you are lost, you'll get by with a little help from those like-minded friends.

If the path to success isn't an easy one, it wasn't meant to be.

Just as a tree needs periodic pruning, your life does as well. The tests and trials you may be put through are life lessons that add to your knowledge and wisdom.

"Often when we fail — assuming we are working diligently — it is because we really are supposed to be doing something else. It means we are on the wrong path. And often that "something else" is so much bigger than what we were doing."

~ SuccessNala at The Abundant Life

Look back over your life and begin to analyze where you seemed to experience the biggest breakthroughs and largest growth. It will most often follow times when you have had a challenge or a set-back. For it is during these testing periods that we naturally begin to think outside the box for our solutions. We then get a new view on life from this angle and unthought-of possibilities open up.

You are a divine being with unlimited energy.

When you fully understand your potential and embrace it, you cannot remain small. You have the essence of your creator within you, which means that you have access to the same power that created the earth, the moon and the stars. When you truly comprehend this idea, you will begin to understand why playing small is simply not an option.

"You have to love what you do. Without passion, great success is hard to come by. An entrepreneur will have tough times if he or she isn't passionate about what they're doing. People who love what they're doing don't give up. It's never even a consideration. It's a pretty simple formula."

~ Donald Trump

As you become comfortable with your God given potential, you will soon realize that you have certain aptitudes and distinct interests. If you follow your inner voice, you will discover that combining your passions with your creative power produces astounding results in your life. Let this built-in guidance system direct you and not only will you meet with success, but with a lifetime of fulfillment as well.

As you play a bigger and bigger game, you are actually expressing gratitude to your creator for this incredible gift called life.

Do not put a ceiling on how high you can go. If you can believe it, you can achieve it. As time worn as that phrase may be, it is as true today as it has ever been.

"Every day in the world someone out there is doing something big, doing something special. When will it be you?"

~ Lou Holtz

To believe is so much more than to simply think about a thing. To believe is to have faith so deep down to your soul that there is no doubt that what you aspire to will happen. So with this in mind, if you knew that you could not fail, what would you do? How could you make that dream even bigger? Try to get rid of all the imagined barriers you have created for yourself and see just how big a game you really can play.

So, are you convinced that it's time to stop playing small? The only one who can keep you from being all that you can be is you. Much of what you have read here you may have already heard before, but have you taken it to heart, have you fully acted upon it? Why not make the decision to take action? Just do it!

Marianne Williamson said it best...

"We ask ourselves, who am I to be brilliant, gorgeous
talented and fabulous?
Actually - who are you not to be?
You are a child of God

Your playing small does not serve the world
There's nothing enlightened about shrinking so that other
people won't feel insecure around you
We are born to make manifest the glory of God that is within us."

Dawn Z. Bournand is a motivating mentor, coach, and international speaker. Her company, Fabulously Successful, is based in Paris, France. With over ten years of teaching and coaching experience, Dawn helps clients realize all that they can possibly be. As a special offer to all Conscious Entrepreneurs, go to www.fabulouslysuccessful.com/SevenPillars.html to claim your free report and sign up for her Fabulously Successful Ezine, or email her at Dawn@FabulouslySuccessful.com for more information.

CHAPTER 2

You are a Master Gardener

Debbi Chambers

*By planting the seed of your goals and intentions, you manifest the dreams
and aspirations of your soul.*

Do you ever find yourself saying "someday" I will achieve my goals?

Most people are willing to wait for the "Perfect" circumstance, sometime in the future, to begin living the life of their dreams. Wishing, hoping or
wanting "It" bad enough will not make it happen.

What is the number one factor that separates those who manifest
their success with grace and ease and the majority of people, who struggle
in quiet desperation? Is it more education, more business opportunities,
good luck, more than 24 hours in each day? The answer may surprise
you...*Setting Goals.*

When I decided to stop trading my precious hours for dollars and become an entrepreneur, I was gifted with this powerful story:

In a Harvard study, the graduates of an MBA program were questioned
on what they intended to accomplish after graduation. 3% of the grads had
set specific, clearly defined and written goals. 13% had goals, but were not
put to paper. 84% had no set goals, save relishing the fact they had graduat-
ed. Ten years later the class was once again polled. The 13% who had goals,

but not clearly defined on paper were earning twice as much as the 84%. The 3% who "took the time" to set specific intentions on what they wanted AND written those clearly defined goals down were earning and enjoying an amazing TEN times the income of 97% of their classmates...combined!

The ONLY difference between the 3% and the 97%, at the start of their career journey was taking the time to set goals.

Our thoughts and dreams are the seeds of our goals we plant in our mental garden. All day. Every day. What we think about we become. Do you desire more prosperity? Plant the seeds of wealth. Is it better health you are seeking? Cultivate seeds of health. Plant your seeds of success. Whenever a thought of doubt, lack or confusion sprout, remind yourself how powerful you are. If you must romance doubt, doubt your limits! Get in the habit of clearing and pulling the negative thoughts (weeds) from your mind.

Gardening Tips

Your goal should be specific to YOU! Always, always put yourself in the picture! For example, if I mention a shiny, new, red Corvette convertible, what is the picture you see in your mind? A shiny, new, red Corvette convertible! But if I say "You are behind the wheel of your shiny, new, red Corvette, with the top down, wind blowing through your hair at sunset", your mental image and emotions change completely. The visualization of the end result will put a smile on your face and joy in your heart. After all, the accomplishment of ANY goal we may have - a new car, a prosperous career, our dream home, a loving relationship - is first and foremost *happiness*. Feel that happiness, feel that gratitude and joy, NOW.

More often than not, we're limited by what we will allow ourselves to receive. This comes from our lack of belief. You absolutely deserve the very best that life has to offer. The following exercise will assist you in discovering your own specific goal.

Start with a clean sheet of paper and draw a line down the middle of it. On the top left side write "My limiting thoughts." On the top right side write: "What I absolutely deserve to be, do and have." On the left side, list the negatives of what you are experiencing or observing. This assists in getting clear on what it is you are seeking to change. Often, just taking the time to get clear on what it is we DO NOT want begins the mental process of change and growth. On the right hand side, next to each limiting circumstance, write exactly what that situation would look like if you could snap your fingers and it would be done. Do not censure your thoughts. Be creative and giving to yourself. Now fold the paper in half length wise, with your "Deservability List" facing up. Take some quiet time to sit with your list. Again, do not censure your thoughts. Entertaining thoughts of the "how's", i.e.: "How will I do that? How will that happen?" are weeds that require pulling! Have faith that all the power in the Universe is working behind the scenes on your behalf. You will begin to resonate with one of your listed desires, and in a short time this "seed" will fill your thoughts and your heart.

Keep your eyes and ears open for clues and opportunities, as they will surely begin to present themselves. As your mental garden blossoms, you will become caught up in the "Divine Spirit" of that which you are manifesting. You become "one" with your goals and desires. Old limitations begin to crumble into the dust they always were. Doors that were once locked shut, not visible or not in your awareness before, will miraculously open. Opportunities, people and events will begin to appear in the most synchronistic of ways. Be prepared to walk through those doors. It will be the right and perfect action for you. Start from where you are, with what you presently have. Science has proven that what we focus on and give our attention to, expands. As we consciously and lovingly nurture our goals seeds, they begin to multiply. We are creators by our very nature. If you look around, you will see that this is true.

The positive impact of setting specific goals, writing them down and making it a daily habit to nurture my dreams has been priceless. No more struggling with the "*what ifs*" and the "*how's.*" I have faith, trust and belief that what I am seeking is seeking me.

"Nothing was in any man that is not in you; no man ever had more spiritual or mental power than you can attain; or did greater things than you can accomplish. You can become what you want to be."
~ WALLACE WATTLES, THE SCIENCE OF BEING GREAT.

We live in an abundant Universe, filled with ideas and riches beyond measure. Love, harmony and abundance are natural states of being. This is true for all people. We are blessed with Infinite Peaceful Possibilities each and every second of each and every day! Start today living the Life You Absolutely DESERVE.

Debbi Chambers, creator of 'Manifesting Garden, Create Your Garden of Infinite Possibilities, A 45 day Goal Achievement Adventure', assists her clients in setting their goals then equips them with confidence, personal power and daily actions steps that move them closer to living the life they desire and DESERVE. Her life transforming 6 week tele-classes in Manifesting Success are a must attend for anyone who is serious about achieving their goals. For more information email her at Debbi@DebbiChambers.com.

CHAPTER 3

It's Never Too Late to Live Your Dream, Your Passion, and Your Joy

Rev. Pat Childers, M.S. in Ed., CEC

To follow your dreams of becoming a spiritual entrepreneur, each person must realize they have something unique and special to share with the world, because they are an individual part of it. Everyone comes into this world connected to "Source." However, each circumstance of every individual's life creates the direction they will take in completing their unique mission and purpose in this life.

I was born an only child, and my parents were very closely connected. This gave me an opportunity to enjoy being their child in the home, but then actually being "my own person" in the world at a very early age. For instance, when I was in grade school, I constantly had other children asking me questions and my opinion about many things, from situations in their families to what they really wanted to do in the world. I would always look into their eyes, feel their feelings, and truly "listen" to them. I eventually had my own "office space" on the playground at recess under a huge sycamore tree. One day a teacher noticed I was not playing dodge ball at recess, but was instead "teaching." I was seven. When she asked me what I was doing, I told her, "I know who I am. I am here on Earth to help people." I told her I was doing the "work," because I was "self-actualized," and was helping everyone else do the same.

Self-actualization occurs when each individual becomes the best person he or she can personally be. Each individual matures and accepts his or her own responsibility for life. At that time, when I was a child, I had not heard of Abraham Maslow, the psychologist who became famous for his hierarchy of human needs. The three stages of "needs" are food and shelter, safety and security, and acceptance by others. He also predicted the transformation of humanity into a realm of spiritual transcendence. In the last sixty years, the percentage of society who is "consciously aware" of assisting with humanity's "spiritual transcendence" has risen from two to twenty percent, and growing every year. Because everyone on the planet has "free will," it is imperative that each individual make a "conscious choice" to accept responsibility for his or her thoughts and actions.

In this state of awareness, transcendence can occur, which leads to unconditional love, altruism, inner joy, a love of nature, the development of intuition, idealism, and a sense of wisdom, which evolves from within. The key is to "know yourself, and what you have to offer in this world." When you follow your own true dreams with passion, others will respect you because you are radiating your "heart center." Everyone will have the opportunity to "see your light." In these times, more people are letting go of the old paradigms, rules, and fear-based teachings from the past. Each person has his or her own unique gifts to share, and can support each other by coordinating and utilizing those gifts as a "universal team." This awareness and awakening allows for clearer choices and independence for "new creative solutions," when choosing to become a spiritual entrepreneur.

In my life, I have had traditional jobs, such as working in a bank, an insurance office, and teaching in the public school system for fifteen years in junior high and high school. I received my certification to teach gifted and talented students, plus my Masters, and also taught some college classes. Then I felt, heard, and knew my calling was to go across the country and connect with many people to expand the universal consciousness. I began connecting locally by putting on metaphysical and holistic fairs in Missouri, writing a column for the Today's Woman magazine, plus many articles in other magazines and newspapers. I became a Reiki Master, an ordained minister, a spiritual life coach, doing many radio and television shows. I continued to expand my connections by being an event coordinator, promoter, networker, and marketer for famous authors and institutes, such as Deepak Chopra, Sylvia Browne, Ted Andrews, Starr Fuentes, Omega Institute, Hay House, International Coach Federation, IPEC, MBS, New Life Expos, Today's Women Shows, INATS, Mishka Productions, and many more.

I now work with individual clients and corporations by teaching, and group coaching for the managers and employees. An example of one of these coaching sessions is:

Team Work/Building Coaching

1. Access their Positive Quotient
2. Get on the team with a shared vision, focus, and purpose
3. Identify the obstacles and negativity that can sabotage the groups' success
4. Develop a system of positive communication and interaction
5. Discover the issues that are holding individuals back from involvement
6. Enhance execution, productivity, and performance
7. Create a customized game plan to renew spirit, enthusiasm, and energy
8. Generate new innovative ideas that stretch thoughts and emotions
9. Expand the awareness of possibilities to reach the "bottom line"

This class provides an over-all view of what is possible, and how the masses can realize it is time to connect to raise the consciousness of humanity to greater and higher achievements. Each entrepreneur needs to link to his or her "true purpose," and then go about creating the most successful strategies of fulfillment for themselves, and their contacts and clients.

This class provides an over-all view of what is possible, and how the masses can realize it is time to connect to raise the consciousness of humanity to greater and higher achievements. Each entrepreneur needs to link to his or her "true purpose," and then go about creating the most successful strategies of fulfillment for themselves, and their contacts and clients.

An important "knowing" on this journey is to be willing to make great associations. It is very beneficial for spiritual entrepreneurs to find people and local organizations that have a special connection to them. Always be ready to ask, "How can we help each other?" Perhaps you could assist each other by putting on combined events, joining through teleseminars, sharing information on each other's web sites, supporting each other as a sponsor, or be a vocal connector by introducing one another to a great niche market to target their information or products. A favorable factor is this does not have to be difficult. It can actually be a lot of fun. It is important to set the intention of exactly what you want, and then "know" it is a successfully completed deal. I truly believe we are all one, and each individual spiritual entrepreneur's idea can fit into the higher picture for good without incurring competition. Each person is also an individual, and has his or her own "unique piece" to bring to the world.

For instance, at the end of last year, I attended a gathering of women where we shared food, gifts, stories, and laughter before we all wrote down exactly what we wanted to let go of from that year, and then set an intention list of all we wanted to acquire in this year. We had a burning bowl ceremony to release the past, and a read out loud connection to enhance our "now" and our "future" of enlightened times. This day provided an expanded view of what is possible.

I truly believe the children arriving today have the knowing, depth, and understanding of their souls' purpose to achieve the predicted transformation of humanity into a realm of spiritual transcendence. It is important that all generations learn to honor and respect each other by sincerely listening and connecting for the greater good. Making sure to follow through in all ways is extremely important. Know that people are wonderful gifts to the Earth and staying connected is fun, rewarding, and helps many other people receive important messages for growth and expansion. Please know it is unwise to be negative. It is important to realize that you could meet your most important significant contact "anywhere." Always be aware, helpful, spontaneous, friendly, and conscious in every situation, while maintaining a positive, upbeat attitude.

"Synchronicity" is very powerful. It is also very powerful to realize that you have assistance from "other realms" whenever you ask. It is your "choice" with your free will to truly "ask and you shall receive." When you share your good energy, it will come right back to you. Do not get so busy just "doing things" that you miss an opportunity to produce a result. As my title indicates, it is never too late to live your dream, so come from your heart in clarity. Be happy now in "each and every" moment. Know it is not too late to live your passion. The famous painter, Grandma Moses, did not start her "art" until she was 67 years old, after being a farmers' wife in New York for years. She was always an inspiration to me as a mentor for fulfilling her life's joy.

So, remember to set your goals and objectives by:
1. Connecting with your soul's purpose in life
2. Mapping out a plan to best serve this mission
3. Doing the work, by following through with your ideas, or products
4. Securing connections for implementation
5. Being fully present when asking assistance to present those items to the world
6. Ask who you can help by being your full self
7. Make a list of what you really want with specific strategies and tactics for on-going success

My mission is to have everyone realize there are no separations, no limits, and no lack of people who are open to what each individual "spiritual entre-preneur" is offering. "Please know there is abundance for all when we work together as a community."

Rev. Pat Childers, M.S. in Ed., CEC, will receive her doctorate, PhD. by completing her new book, The Indigo Grandmother, Communication Among the Generations *to be submitted to Hay House as directed by Louise Hay. Pat will be able to reach many different people by connecting to a variety of venues when speaking at seminars and conferences across the country. Contact Pat by phone, 417-859-4963, e-mail, patchilders1111@yahoo. com, mail, 1022 Roanoke, Marshfield, Missouri 65706, or visit her website, www.PatChilders.com.*

CHAPTER 4

Is That God Talking?
Find Your Solutions Easily Through
Your Own Inner Guidance

Diane Eisenman, M.A., M.Div.

Despite all the advice you receive from experts and friends as you create and grow your business, you are the bottom line. Who do you listen to and trust when you make important decisions about your projects? You might ask yourself:

- What are all the facts?
- Is this the right time?
- Will I be happy with this decision?
- Am I able to carry out the new responsibilities?
- Does this decision engage my passion?
- How would I feel if I made a different decision?

The answers to these questions lie within your own inner life. The bigger question is, how do you go about finding them?

Listening to Others

Soliciting facts from others is helpful when you need to gather information. It is also useful to collect opinions from friends and family, especially those who might be directly affected by your decisions. An insightful listener can be a mirror to see your situation more clearly, reflecting back to you your authentic truth.

However, advisors are necessarily limited by their own experience and beliefs. They have their own levels of personal risk factors, comfort zones, and priorities. Their advice is based on their own history, feelings, and understanding. Seeing the situation through their own filters, they declare, "If I were you, this is what I'd do."

Listening to God

But – they are not you. At times, you need to turn to a more objective voice, one that knows you more intimately than even you know yourself, and that you can trust beyond all others. This is the voice of God, the source and creator of your life. Whether you feel God is something other than yourself, or is the life stream pulsing within you; whether you name this voice Spirit, Inner Being, Source, or Creator, this God created you with unique gifts to attract health, wealth, and happiness. Your Creator wants you to become the most successful person that you can imagine. You only need ask, and listen for your answers.

Answers absolutely come when you surrender to your true mission. Your passion compels you to make the choices that feel best to you. Once you have really committed yourself and step onto the path, the law of attraction brings you what you need. Your new life will come easily if your desire is strong, your thoughts are focused, and your image is clear.

Messages from God

Your Source "speaks" to you in many ways.

- **Hunches:** When you have a sudden inspired thought that you "know" is just right, you feel a great sense of relief. You might feel an urge to call a customer at just the right moment. You confidently order 1,000 extra books, not knowing if you will sell them. Where do these thoughts come from?
- **Dreams:** Through your dreams, answers come, and choices are made without having to live them out in this physical world. Often symbols are revealed that illuminate deeper parts of your truth. By writing down

your dreams, you discover helpful new perspectives from a source beyond your conscious self.

- **Coincidences:** The timing of seemingly unrelated events often contains powerful messages. A problem might have you stumped until an unexpected encounter offers a surprise solution. Perhaps a song on the radio gives you a new idea. These coincidences give you hope and confidence that you are being guided by a Source larger than your personal will.

- **Life Experiences:** Wisdom is imbedded in your daily mistakes and successes. Ultimately experience teaches us that change is the only way to sustain life – you grow as you receive new impulses, and manifest them. You also grow as you let go of what is no longer needed or useful. When you refuse to take a chance on the new, or hold on to the old, you find yourself stuck. As you embrace these opposing directions, you maintain a balance in the present moment. The challenge is to both create and release simultaneously to avoid the wild oscillations of the pendulum.

When God Speaks

You recognize God speaking when you get chills, or you experience an immense sense of relief. You feel better. You feel the excitement and possibility of creating something that truly comes from your deep passion. You feel connected with something much greater than yourself. You find hope again, and realize that life is very good! You are ready to move forward, leave your stuck place, and take the next step to growing and transforming your business and your life. You implement your vision with a focus, clarity, and enthusiasm that is unstoppable.

How Can You Be a Better Listener?

Messages from Source are being sent all the time. Here are three simple practices to help diffuse the distractions around you and allow your inner guidance to "speak." Take a "Source Break" instead of a coffee break, and you will quickly have access to a vast world of new resources. The trick is to move past your own ego-centered filters for a moment, and trust your deeper wisdom to reveal itself. And be ready to capture that wisdom when it comes!

Practice #1 - Quieting Your Mind

Every spiritual tradition teaches simple practices that quiet and center the mind to make room for grander visions. Religions call these practices prayer, meditation, mantra, or chanting. Others call them relaxation exercises, breath work, or toning. All of these methods use the power of breath, rhythm, and vibration to eliminate distracting thoughts and enter into the essence of Source.

Breath is a simple and safe way to easily quiet your thoughts and focus on that greater space within you. Simply find a quiet space, and just breathe. Sit comfortably and focus on the inhalation and exhalation of your breath. Close your eyes to eliminate visual distraction, and just feel the movements of your breath, in and out, rising and falling, expanding and contracting, taking in and letting go. Let your breath flow naturally, and notice the rhythm of breath soothe and calm your busy mind. At some point you may have no thoughts at all, just an awareness of pure space. It is from this still place that your inner voice can be heard.

Practice #2 - Writing Spontaneously

As children, many of us kept a diary. Now as adults, we still need a place to safely express our stories, feelings, hopes and fears. Letting one sentence lead to the next, write spontaneously, not knowing where your thoughts will lead. Writing itself brings emotional relief. Write without judgment or criticism, celebrating that you are alive and experiencing life's lessons. By expressing your thoughts and feelings through writing, you witness your life objectively, discovering the wisdom it contains. These reflections guide you closer to where you want to be.

Writing is free and easy. Here are some suggestions to get you started:

- Ask yourself a question and then answer it.
- Vent your current frustrations – no censoring allowed!
- Imagine your perfect life.
- Discuss what is getting in the way of your highest vision.
- Note something that you are grateful for today.

What is important is that you take paper and pen in hand and write. Start with a deep breath, and then let your heart lead you. Stop if you find yourself trying to "figure it out," and wait in that silent pause for words to come. Let go of your inhibitions, and let your Source reveal your thoughts to you.

Practice #3 - Finding Inspiration

What makes you feel inspired - a good book, a great piece of music, a heart-warming story? Perhaps listening to a motivational speaker moves you to action. If you look, you will find many little moments of inspiration come to you, if you would but capture them and allow them to lift you. Encouragement from an employee or gratitude from a customer can make your day. Take time to enjoy these moments when life feels good, when you are participating in the sacred nature of life, when little miracles come your way.

Choose to live an inspired life. You can fret about what is "wrong" with your world, or instead, you can choose to appreciate what is working "right", and look for more ways to bring joy and abundance into your life and your business. Be refreshed by a visit to nature. Choose friends who encourage you and are manifesting their own creative ideas.

Listening with Your Senses

Let your senses move you to action. Surround yourself with beauty, sweet smells, delicious tastes, things soft and warm. Display your favorite art. Listen to uplifting music. Check out the sensory experience of your business. Does your environment appear chaotic or calm? What sounds do you hear? How does your company "taste?" What smells are in the air? Does your company feel warm or cold? Does your physical space enhance your capabilities or your limitations?

Answers from your Source are available to you if you but stay awake and be receptive! Your God is calling you. Will you hear?

*Diane Eisenman, M.A., M.Div., spiritual counselor, educator, and music maker, assists you to deepen your connection with God through music, imagery, and insight. She offers consultations and self-study courses to awaken your inner listening, so you will be ready when God speaks to you. Go to InnerGuidanceCounseling.com to receive **Inspired Moments** for free weekly tips, and accept a special complimentary report. She can be reached at 877-212-5894, or P.O. Box 381, Verdugo City, CA 91046.*

CHAPTER 5

Embracing The Paradigm Shift: Creating the Conscious Space Between Where You Are and Where You Are Going

Sherry Gaba,
Licensed Clinical Social Worker and Life Coach

I have learned the key to being a Conscious Entrepreneur is by letting go of fears and attachments; celebrating the process by living mindfully, and embracing my intuition. This is where the transformation began. This is when I was called forth to make the paradigm shift from where I was... to where I was going.

I remember the moment when this shift enfolded in my life. I was sitting at a staff meeting and this inner knowingness arrived saying, "You can't do this anymore." Ordinarily, the "good girl" would tap me on the shoulder to say, "You can't leave your job! What will you do?" or "How will you make a living?" Once the truth revealed itself to me, there was no turning back. I left the job and started my own business. Living an authentic life, I discovered, transforms you. Your integrity, creativity, essence, vitality, and life force becomes alive. You will not be able to hold off the excitement and sense of infinite possibilities that await you. You are finally living values that resonate within your core. You are no longer answering to "I should do this," or "I am supposed to be doing that," because you are finally letting go of endless chatter you have internalized that no longer fit the person you are becoming.

Letting go of fear

Loosening the grip on your fears keeps the focus on your goals and the divine creative process. Fear breeds envy for what other's have and what you lack. Instead, allow for acceptance of others and you will be rewarded with increased profits and a flourishing business. How? Because you are attracting back what you have given to others. You cannot be in harmony with the universe if your thoughts are paralyzed in anxiety. Fear robs you of feeling gratitude for the abundance you already possess and have yet to realize. One way to eliminate fear is knowing it is a habitual way of coping with what is uncomfortable. This was imprinted in you a long time ago from parents, society, religious institutions, and the environment. Living in fear is counterproductive because it is a prelude for scarcity. Scarcity is negative energy manifested by fearful thinking. By unraveling these destructive distortions, you unlock the door to prosperity, abundance, and self-acceptance. As a Conscious Entrepreneur, anxiety will only attract anxious people into your life and business. If important decisions are rooted in fear, others will feel your desperation and neediness. They will not be interested in buying your product or signing up for your services. I had a client who was starting a jewelry design business who felt stuck wondering what would happen if she wasn't successful. I pointed out to her she already was a success by following her dreams. Once she believed in herself, the universe brought her exactly what she needed for her business to grow. She began to apply positive affirmations to her daily regimen, and practiced guided visualizations of running a successful jewelry empire, and eventually her desires became a reality. By taking these steps, she began getting orders from major department stores wanting her designs.

Tools for letting go of fears

Affirm daily "I release all fears that haunt me." Purge feelings related to fear of failure, the unknown, and rejection when they arise. Journal critical fear based thoughts with energizing, non-judgmental ones.

Affirmations hold, create, and declare all that is available to you. By putting these intentions out there, they more likely will manifest.

Letting go of attachments

Have you ever received a gift from someone or a check for your business and instead of feeling joyful, you felt empty? I call that the "More" disease - that aching feeling that enough is never enough. That is because the more 'stuff' you accumulate, the more you want. You have this insatiable appetite for more and more. This is because you not only define yourself by what you have, but are constantly in fear of losing it! You believe more 'stuff' is what you need to succeed. However, what you are doing is blocking your energy field with neediness, desperation and greed, which will ultimately attract your worst fears back to you. It is through letting go of these desperate needs that you free yourself from attachment. When you chose to live in the 'always wanting for more' mentality, you lose the ability to be grateful for what you do have. You stop living in the "being" and live in the "having." This type of neediness distracts you from accomplishing your goals and blocks the universal flow for that which you desire. By going into a space of serenity, you attract business from a state of grace and harmony, rather than from a place of anxiety and fear. By doing the footwork and staying out of the results, the universe brings you exactly what you and your clients need. You no longer need to over sell what you offer, or push yourself on to others. This will only be seen as manipulation and desperation. Start listening to the underlying messages of what your clients really need, make connections, point out their strengths and weaknesses when relevant, and bring your spirit into all your interactions. Clients and customers will feel the divine difference between authenticity and desperate attachment.

Tools for letting go of attachments

Affirm daily "I let go of attachments allowing the universe to bring me what I need."

Donate something of yours to others more in need. The rewards are immeasurable.

Want less and enjoy the process rather than living in the outcome. Keep a gratitude book in which you can write your thanks every day.

Celebrating the process by living mindfully

This stage is where the creative process begins to percolate. This is not about crunching numbers or developing a business plan, but rather celebrating each step whether it is productive or not. This is the time when the vision finds you. You begin to notice and get curious with what is already surrounding you. Suddenly your vision is crystal clear and appears as a byproduct of life's unfolding process. This is when success is not dependent on some future event or far off distant dream. Celebrating the process occurs by living mindfully in an awakened state here and now. You become the observer of your life and can see things from a distance and 'outside the box.' By doing this, you avoid getting stuck in a limited perspective, making room for your divine creativity to incubate. . Your business becomes a mind, body, and soul activity. You engage all your senses into the decisions you make and stop trying to outsmart the universe. Gems of epiphanies appear, and you become aware of what your clients need, which in turn, allows you to be more effective. Your self-awareness makes you more empathic. People appear and ideas flourish when you chose to be present. Resources and unexpected referrals show up when you are mindful and decisions are made easily and organically. This is cosmic law.

Tools for celebrating the process mindfully.

Affirm daily "By being mindful, I allow for opportunities to appear."

Every time you reach a milestone, celebrate.

Allow creativity to flow in the ordinary nuisances of your daily life.

Use meditation, introspection, and self-reflection to increase conscious awareness. Design a prosperity wheel, collage, or a journal, to remind you of the unlimited possibilities that await you.

Embrace your intuition

Intuition is taking your mind and thoughts out of the equation and replacing them with the universe's wisdom. This is when you take your ego out of the mix and experience the natural flow of your own essence. When you learn to rely on this guidance, your business ventures will flow with an effortless quality. The endless chatter will be replaced with your higher self's wisdom letting you know exactly what you need to do. Life is always sending us messages, and by being conscious, these messages speak to us, if we are willing to listen. If your sixth sense is telling you to change direction in your business, listen to it. When you give yourself the time to be still, gems of wisdom appear, giving you exactly what you need exactly when you need it. Unleash your 'GPS' system to set free the limitless pure potentiality of possibilities that awaits you.

Tools for embracing your intuition:

Affirm daily, "My life force, through its abundant wisdom, is always available to me."

Meditate 10 minutes a day giving your intuition an opportunity to speak.

Sing, chant, play music, or move your body to allow for states of consciousness to shift. Participate in guided meditation, visualizations or breathing exercises.

Why not begin running your business free of fear and attachments? Revel in your successes by creating a business mindfully and with profound intuition. Prosperity, including money, is a form of living energy. It obeys the law of cause and effect with pure consciousness drawn from the universe and manifested into the physical world. A conscious business is the materialization of that energy form, and when you operate your business in this way, you are spreading the spiritual laws of abundance to yourself and more importantly, throughout the world where it is needed most. Therefore, Cosmic Law welcomes your success. Aligning yourself with abundance is the ultimate gift of giving and receiving the blessings of the universe.

Sherry Gaba, Life Coach and Licensed Psychotherapist (LCSW), believes awareness is a prerequisite to change. What you perceive, determines your reality. Sherry's clients have achieved success by discovering their own paradigm of possibilities. Sherry believes success is not something you aspire to, but something that already exists within you, waiting to be realized. Email her at sherry@sgabatherapy.com or call 818-756-3338. Her website is www.sgabatherapy.com. Contact her to receive a free monthly newsletter and a free consultation.

CHAPTER 6

Driving Through Life With the Brakes On: End Procrastination Once and For All

Linda Keefe

Have you ever put off doing something that, if you just did it, could have significant implications for your business?

I know I have. One of my most recent "procrastination challenges" was submitting the application to become an approved vendor for the US Federal Government as a management consultant and trainer. That's huge!

So, what did I do for two and a half years? I put it off. I spent some time working on it in bits and pieces, trying to get it just right, but mostly I didn't move heaven and earth to finish it.

Okay, eventually I got it done. Hooray! But how much revenue did that procrastination cost me? How much missed opportunity for dealing with the "big guns" did I lose? We'll never know, but one thing for sure is that I can't get it back. And neither can you.

So the real question becomes, how many *other* things am I putting off that could mean huge returns for me and my business? How can I learn *not* to procrastinate on the important stuff?

If you're like me, I found a whole slew of things – once I started to really notice them. Do any of these strike a chord with you?

- Is there a proposal that you wanted to put together?
- Have you been meaning to organize your office files?

- Do you owe a chapter draft for an aggregated book? (Okay, so now you know writing this for you fell into my "procrastination" pile.)

What is on *your* list – and why do you put these things off?

The first reason that comes to mind is because they are so important! While that may be true, what are the underlying reasons? There are all kinds of them. We may think:

- There's not enough time.
- I have to get it just right.
- My creative muse isn't on board.
- It's too hard.
- I don't know how to get started.

Do you see what is really going on here?

We have *negative* thoughts in our mind about: 1) how much time it will take, or 2) how capable we are of doing it. Does this match with your thoughts?

Moving Forward With Full Force

The good news is that you can convert any and all procrastination-driving thoughts into powerful, forward-moving actions!

Imagine fearlessly going forward on vital projects, taking the steps that can bring you fame and fortune!

Can you see yourself bringing in more jobs, getting them done expeditiously, and being praised for your remarkable results? How would you feel when you go through the day, the week, the month, knowing that everything is working smoothly, ahead of schedule and top-notch?

That would be wonderful, wouldn't it? Does it seem like a dream? Something almost unattainable?

If I told you ONE thing you could do to end procrastination and inertia in your business once and for all, would you try it? Sure, you say! YES!

But before I tell you, I'm going to ask you not to pooh-pooh it until you've read the rest of the chapter and given it a chance. I know it works. I use it every day, and it never fails.

Thought Is Tangible, Material Substance

It has to do with your thoughts. Yes, I know you already realize that what you think is what you get, and that is all fine and well, but did you know that *thought is material substance?*

This is key! Thought is actually *matter* – physical substance. Something theoretically that you could reach out and touch. It's not just an elusive idea or a non-thing. It is, and has, material substance. It's a tangible entity. All matter follows the laws of physics. And *thought is matter*.

We know this to be true from the studies in quantum physics that have proven its molecular structure and energy fields. We know *thought is material substance* also from experiences like those with Betty in the book *Across The Unknown* by Stewart Edward White. She is fervently told from the other side that, "thought is matter." We are told that we must respect it as such and treat the knowledge of that fact as the answer to all our problems – the means to realizing all we desire. *Thought is material substance.*

The implication here for our business lives is huge. If what you *think* creates physical matter, then might we want to be more careful with what we have in our minds?

We can't afford any negative or doubtful thoughts. We don't want that energy, that material substance, hanging around in our businesses. No longer do we have the luxury of thinking of *anything* we don't want. That means no worrying about when the bills are going to be paid; no fears of losing a bid to a competitor; no doubting our ability to present a dynamite speech to a critical crowd.

So what can we do? How can we use this new knowledge to change our world in little -- and magnificent –pervasive ways?

Consciously Create Thought Clouds

You've heard everyone from Robert Anthony to Joe Vitale, (and of course Norman Vincent Peale), tout the wonders of positive thinking. Now you know *why* this works. It's not just a matter of thinking things and they will magically appear, it is the fact that *thought is material substance*. It IS your reality. So let's get vigilant and go through a three step process for cleaning up your thought closet.

Step #1: Take a Thought Inventory

Take charge of your thoughts! Assiduously guard your mind from letting anything in that may reek of negativity. You have to be careful, because those little doubts and fears have a way of sneaking in when you least expect them, even in the most positive and confident person's mind. What about the thought, "I have so much to do, I'll never get it done". "I'm too fat." "That's going to be difficult to do."

Do an inventory of your thoughts for a while and see what you come up with. Be cognizant of what goes on in the back of your mind. As you go through your day, notice the subliminal thoughts you have about what is and is not getting done.

Be honest with yourself. You'll have to take the optimistic spin off your thinking for a while to just notice what is really going on. Is there a part of you that thinks you're not quite up to the task? What is your reason for not taking on a project? How do you really feel about making a follow up call to a prospect about a new account? Notice how many times you have a slightly doubtful or fearful slant on getting something done.

Step #2: Flip The Negative Into A Positive

Once you've identified all the negative thought seeds you've been planting along the way, define what you want and flip the negative into a positive. For instance:

- Move from, "I'll never get all these papers on my desk put away" to "*I can file these in a breeze – I'm an organized person.*"
- Stop telling yourself, "I'll never catch up" to "*I'm on top of everything I need to do.*"
- Switch from, "I bet my prospect has not called me because he has decided against the project" to "*I'm going to call him because he's anxious to get started and he needs my help.*"
-

I could create an endless list, but you get the drift. I guarantee that once you start being on the lookout for your sub thoughts and how they are limiting you, you will be astounded.

Step #3: Encase Yourself In A Thought Cloud

Now comes the fun part. It's not just a matter of thinking new thoughts. You want to encase yourself, (and the world immediately around you), in a thought cloud of *your* choosing.

In my mind, I create a mini *thought cloud* that encircles me. It moves wherever I go. Like you see in cartoons where someone walks around with a rain cloud over his head, and everywhere he goes the cloud stays with him. Literally picture your thoughts being the umbrella for everyone around you.

This is what you want to do with your thoughts when you come to a specific situation – create thought clouds. While what you think all day long is important, you can use the reality that *thought is material substance* and surround yourself with super-charged thought in "tense" situations. For instance, when you're calling a prospect, wrap yourself with the thoughts of what you want the outcome to be.

Or perhaps you're dealing with a difficult employee. Wrap yourself in the result you want before talking to him or her by creating a thought cloud of it being a productive, beneficial discussion. Because *thought is material substance*, you don't have the luxury of harboring the idea that the employee is giving you problems. If you do, that will become your reality – because thought *is* matter.

Your thoughts rule your life and your business. Make them what you want!

Linda Keefe, "The Execute Your Vision Maven", publishes the 'Execute Your Vision: Strategies and Tools' weekly ezine. Discover little known secrets to success by tapping into your inner self and leveraging online entrepreneurship.

*If you are ready to jump-start your business, become independently wealthy, and have more freedom in life, go to **www.ExecuteYourVision.com** for a FREE Teleseminar Audio: "How To Make A Fortune ($$$) On The Internet With Information Marketing." Contact Linda at LindaKeefe@SharedResults. com or call 888-689-8077.*

CHAPTER 7

The Seven States of the Conscious Entrepreneur

Michael L. Mead

All entrepreneurs begin with the idea they are creating something visible in the world. Whether it's an innovative product or business strategy, a sizeable bank account or a building with your name on it, you expect something big and wonderful to show up out there in the world.

For conscious entrepreneurs, your business is an outward reflection of your internal journey. What's of real enduring value shows up "in here" – in your own consciousness, your way of being. Sure, all the stuff "out there" is pleasurable and exciting, and contributes to the well being of others, but who you become along the way is the real payoff.

You create value for others by transforming yourself. Your business becomes a mirror of who you are becoming and prosperity is inevitable. Entrepreneurship is the most accurate and dynamic feedback system ever created for observing how your transformation is unfolding.

Certain ways of being, or states of consciousness, are leverage points in the development process. By intentionally developing these states in yourself, you will naturally develop business vitality. The seven leverage points of consciousness are compassion, curiosity, congruence, commitment, character, capacity and collaboration. Although you may know the words, my explanation of these states of being point to a whole new paradigm of business.

Compassion: The state of perceiving every person, interaction and event as your creation. You accept what's so without argument, and embrace every situation as Spirit inviting you home.

Compassion is the most overlooked quality of entrepreneurship, a grace you give yourself and others. Either you are the "cause" in your life and your business, or you are the "effect." Being the effect stands on the thought "I am powerless in the face of this circumstance." Being the cause is an empowering context in which you have the power to transform yourself, your business, and even others.

As cause, you recognize that you created everything, consciously and unconsciously – from the person with whom you are interacting to the problem you are addressing. With compassion for yourself and your creations, you can easily forgive yourself and others, surrendering any limitation to Spirit.

Accept your powerful and creative nature. Your life and business will transform.

Curiosity: The state of "not knowing;" the liberator from the tyranny of judgment.

Business comes at you like a bullet fired from a gun at point-blank range, fast and furious. No matter how much you plan, plans fall apart at the point of engagement. The infamous heavy weight champion Mike Tyson nailed it: "Every fighter has a plan – until he gets hit."

Most entrepreneurs learn to respond to the "hit" by making quick decisions and relying on gut reactions. Curiosity, on the other hand, requires a pause.

Curiosity is waiting for your second, third, or thirtieth response to see which one is in flow. It's letting go and waiting rather than having the ready answer. It's the willingness to stand in the face of inaction until Spirit delivers the answer to you.

As I write this, I can approach the task from knowing what to say or from curiosity. Whenever I approach from knowing, I work hard searching my mind's database. Writing becomes an effort. I search harder; less surfaces. As less surfaces, I work harder.

Then, I lean back in my chair, take a few deep breaths and ask Spirit to guide me. I have no idea what is coming. Each word flows. I'm as surprised about what I say as you are.

Stand in "not knowing" and ask Spirit for guidance. Your possibilities will expand.

Congruence: The state where your business is a full expression of your true nature.

Entrepreneurship is performing art without a script. Just like any form of art, it is an expression of Spirit manifested in space/time geometry.

Your business will have optimal vitality when it is the expression of your true and essential nature. This essential part of your self is already within you.

You cannot find it by looking within your mind. You will only find there what you were programmed to do – by education, background, parenting, culture, etc. You will find your Spirit by opening to your being, that part of you where your energy naturally expands when you move in a particular direction.

My mind directed me from college to law school to investment banking. I excelled until I became successful. Then I hit the "This ain't it" brick wall. As I look back, I pursued the path of business for everyone but me.

When I hit the wall, I wandered around like Moses for over a decade. With enough "desert," – the clear space of reflection, meditation, opening to flow, feedback from those who loved me – I found my Spirit.

It shocked me: I'm a spiritual teacher. How I know this as fact is that my energy moves me toward it. I don't move it; it moves me.

With congruence, your business moves itself easily and consistently with who you are.

Commitment: The state where you operate beyond your applied resources; the manifested expression of your desire.

When I first began to succeed in the business world, it seemed I had a magic wand. I would declare what I wanted to create, commit all my resources to it, and "voila!" – there it appeared.

When my boom abruptly went bust, my reaction to my mounting failures was to increase my commitment – applying more time, more intelligence, more sweat.

Imagine if you will that you take your head and beat it against a cement wall for a while. You don't get a dented wall. You get a bashed head.

Wobbly and bleeding, I noticed that applying more resources wasn't working. I began to ask myself, "What do I really want? What moves me? What does my heart desire?"

When I discovered the answer, my old definition of commitment became irrelevant. It revealed itself as an external tool to compensate for a lack of internal desire. With internal desire ignited, I operate beyond commitment. My energy naturally flows into my business.

Giving free rein to your desire is the commitment that produces results.

Character: The state of service where you see other's well being as your own.

I was a multi-millionaire by my early thirties. During that arrogant span of my life, I ordered people around. "I'm the boss and you'd better know it." I was on top!

Luckily, Spirit was gracious enough to humble me. I went from a big bank account to no bank account, from a big house and three cars to no house or cars.

While on the bottom, I met a teacher who taught me service. He put me in what I considered a menial job, serving food and cleaning houses – for no pay. From CEO to unpaid servant – what a fall!

He showed me how to transcend my judgments about the job and give myself to others. I opened. The concept that we are **One** was now an actual experience.

Serve others. You will develop character; you can't help but follow the Golden Rule.

Capacity: The state of opening to your innate resources and directing those resources to create your desires.

Most entrepreneurs confuse capital with capacity. My investment banking days taught me that. Others confuse competence with capacity.

Capital and competence and most other external conditions, are effects of capacity – not the cause. Capacity for the conscious entrepreneur is an opening in the mind/body that allows resources – internal and external – to flow. To increase your capacity you will have to open ... let go ... make space in your being to flow more energy, attention, consciousness, and information.

Open your mind/body to flow and all necessary resources will appear.

Collaboration: The state that allows the innate desire of each person to be the energy that drives your business.

What I've learned about working with others to produce a result is paradoxical to conventional thinking. If you look under all the talk about organizational development, conventional wisdom says you "motivate" or "move" someone to do something you want.

A former partner once complained, "If you can get a circus elephant to walk around in a circle, why can't you get people to do what you want?"

Great question! After years of struggle and effort, I found the answer. It's so simple that it defies the intellect. Find out what people **want** to do. If they want to do what you want done, then you have a match for your team. No more motivation, inspiration, demanding or pleading – just collaboration.

How you find out what they want to do is ask them and watch. If their energy moves when they say "yes," you have a match. If not, move on.

Recently, someone on my team was not performing to my desire. The conventional response was to fire or change. Instead, I gently, but persistently asked for what I wanted and watched to see if it was what she wanted. Quickly it became obvious she did not want the same thing and resigned voluntarily, a bigger fan of our business than ever.

Collaboration with people's innate desires will tap into a powerful force for moving your business forward easily and naturally.

Conscious entrepreneurship is about who you are and who you become. Grow in each of the 7 "C's" and you will be delighted with yourself and your business.

Michael L. Mead is a former lawyer, investment banker, venture capitalist and serial entrepreneur. Spirit graciously landed Michael, despite his ego's fighting objection, in a business dedicated to people living in their spiritual nature. He contributed to the development of the Technology of Stillness®, a set of practices and principles that open the body and quiet the mind so you can easily and predictably tap into your Source. Go to www.LivingInStillness. com or contact Michael at michael@LivingAtEase.com or (888) 221-5475.

CHAPTER 8

Silver-Platter Consciousness™

Christine E. Michel

No matter who I meet, I get asked the same question over and over again, "Christine, how do you do it? How do you stay in that place of pure joy? How do you stay in the place of peace and harmony knowing your next steps are being revealed to you?" What is the secret, the technique? What's the process?" It's trust. Just trust that you are reading this because you are open to hearing a simple Truth, and what you came here for is exactly what you are going to receive.

As an entrepreneur, it is my responsibility to have the most amazingly successful conscious business by living my best life now. I lead by example, unattached to the results or outcome, and not to convince others of my way. By simply being a loving, joyful example of what is possible and available to all of us, I successfully do what I came here to do. It is my responsibility to be the beautiful example of prosperity: more to all - less to none. There is more than enough abundance; for example, clients, money, speaking engagements, to go around. I live by my philosophy of 'Silver-Platter Consciousness™', where everyone was born with a Silver Platter overflowing with all good.

One day I had a vision wherein God handed me a Silver Platter filled with all of life's possibilities and asked me, "Christine, what will you have?" In that instant I knew that everything I could ever need, want or desire in a lifetime was on this platter. For the first time in my life I said, "I'll take it all God. Thank You, thank You, thank You." Then God said to me, "It has always been here, it always will be, and by the way, each and every one of you has an overflowing Silver Platter. By accepting your own infinite abundance, you don't take away from anyone else's." It is up to each and every one of us to choose all good, right now, from this overflowing Silver Platter that is simply brimming over with infinite possibilities.

This mindset completely eliminates the idea of competition and fear that there isn't 'enough' to go around. I can't take anything away from anyone as I express my unique way of being in my business. Knowing this *does* set you free. All of the worry, stress, and anxiety of a competitive existence fade away. The Conscious Entrepreneur (CE) does not worry whether or not someone else is doing better than they are. The CE does not worry if someone wants to copy them or emulate them in any way. The CE knows that there is more than 'enough' for everyone, and that their way of being is their unique thumbprint. Therefore there is no begging, borrowing or stealing. You can't take something away from someone that is their own style.

Take Ownership

Whether I am working one-on-one with a client or inspiring a full audience, I do it from the place of having everything I could ever desire and more, doing that which I love. When someone shows up who is more successful than I am, I see this as an opportunity for me to own those very qualities that are being reflected to me. We are each little hand-held mirrors for one another, simply showing each other what is possible, both negative and positive. I truly celebrate when I become aware that I am feeling envy, jealousy or admiration for another, because this allows me to ask myself "What am I thinking or feeling?" If I feel envy or jealousy, it is because I am thinking from a place of lack. I am feeling as though he/she has something that I don't have, which, of course, is never true. You cannot see something in another that is not within you! Now I can look at my limited beliefs, transform them and own the very qualities that I disowned to begin with. The same goes for admiration. If I am admiring someone's way of being or their success, I now have the opportunity to own those qualities and be more of what I am attracted to in another. Oprah Winfrey and Ellen Degeneres have always been good examples of this for me. When I looked at all the qualities these women were being: loving, generous, creative, kind, successful, persistent, competent, confident, tenacious, vivacious, compassionate, speaking from the heart, humorous, and caring just to name a few; I was able to own those qualities and bring them into all areas of my life as a way of being. What do you want more of in your life or your business? Whatever it is, be it! When I was in college I remember being envious of a woman in my Marketing Club. She was outgoing, beautiful, confident, always presentable, articulate and the list goes on and on. When I became aware of how I was feeling, rather less than, I committed myself to looking at her as an example of what I truly was and started being those qualities. It is really quite simple and this is where some people get even more distracted; they think that success 'should' be more difficult. The truth is always simple!

Parallel Universes

It is our responsibility to be the best we can be in this moment and in all ways. I believe that infinite parallel universes exist at the same time. Any idea or question that you have is answered right now as you tap into the *you* that is already experiencing it or knows the answer. You can tap into the global consciousness at the same time and ask the answer to come forward from another who knows. I invite you to tap into the parallel universe where you are already successful - being, doing and having all that you could ever desire. Anything that comes up that does not fit in with your idea of success, for example, fear, doubt, worry, limiting beliefs, resistance, - comes up to be transformed, not to hold you back. These limiting beliefs are not validation that you can't be successful and thrive in a conscious business; they simply come forward because they no longer serve you and it is your job to be diligent and do the work of reframing, transforming, uplifting yourself and your consciousness.

So many of my clients have benefited from the concept of parallel universes. One of them who was looking for his soul mate stopped looking 'out there somewhere in the future' and realized that his soul mate was already here in a parallel universe, living a very abundant life with him right now. He began tapping into the Self that was already having this successful relationship, and began speaking, acting, and being the soul mate that he was looking for. Imagine how powerful this is! You no longer project or visualize something out in the future; you now realize that you are already living the kind of life that you thought you were only dreaming of. Another client desired to take her business to a new level of success. I shared with her the concept of parallel universes. I told her that simply having the idea that she wanted to have increased success came from the Self that was already experiencing increased success in a parallel universe. All she had to do was tap into this Self having the business success that she desired and be open to knowing her next steps. She is well on her way!

Guidance is all around you. Your next step is revealed in the song on the radio; in the conversation you overhear in the grocery store; on the billboard advertisement; in the flash of insight that you might not normally pay attention to. Pay attention! Think of a favorite quote that has always inspired you. I have many and one of my favorites is a quote from the Bible. "*I am the light of the world. Whoever follows me will not walk in darkness, but have the light of life.*" - John 8:12. This is my life commitment. I know as I follow the Light of the Truth within, I can never be lost. Bringing this philosophy into my business, I am committed to being a Light for my clients, for my audiences, and inspiring others to be the Light for themselves and the world.

Christine Michel holds a Master's in Spiritual Psychology. She is a certified Transformational Life Coach and Inspirational Speaker, and has a private practice wherein she assists people in transforming their lives and living in Silver-Platter Consciousness™. She invites you to affirm your truth consistently, stick to it diligently, and live your infinite possibilities now. Life the way you always desired it to be! Call 805/331-1122, email Christine@ LivingVisionsCoaching.com, or visit www.LivingVisionsCoaching.com.

CHAPTER 9

Conscious Manifestation

David Neagle

Have you ever really desired something, but you were unsure as to how to get it? More often than not, I receive questions from students as to "HOW" they should go about manifesting their desires. Many say they want to learn HOW to manifest more money, deep passions, more business clients, relationships, financial freedom, adventurism and romanticism, better health, great sex, their life's purpose & so on..., but just how do you get from point A to point B?

The short-cut to discovering the "Path of HOW" is to first look at why you're asking yourself those questions in the first place. The truth is, this question originates from within an individual and is at the core of what he or she legitimately wants and is supposed to experience in his or her lifetime. "HOW" questions represent the root of a person's passions. By trying to determine how to achieve a particular goal, we're actually drawing attention to what we really want. Think of it this way – if a person asks, *"What can I do to reach my financial goals?"* or *"How do I find my soul-mate?"* it's a strong indicator that what the person really wants is financial freedom and a lifelong partner.

It's great that you have identified your desires, but be cautious of the way in which you construct your questions, because it can lead you down a dead end road where you never reach your goals or fulfill your desires.

The KEY to getting what you want is to understand that you already possess the power and ability to manifest what you want to have and experience. For those of you that are students of the Law of Attraction, this idea requires that you now prepare yourself to step up and become even more aware of your true innate power on a much deeper level.

Attraction indicates separation between you and the thing you want. Rather than focus on attracting your desires (or drawing in an experience that is separate from you), it's much faster to gain an understanding of the power of "Conscious Manifestation." To do so, you must remove the idea of separateness, thus forgetting about attracting anything. Think of it instead as "Instant Creation."

To really grasp the power of Conscious Manifestation, you MUST let go of an imaginary idea - the concept of time. Whether you realize it or not, you are instantly creating everything you are experiencing in your life right now. Your past and your future can only exist in your imagination and manifestation can only exist in the now. NOW is the only thing that is real, and because most people are afraid to fully experience "NOW," they spend most of their lives living in the past or living in the future.

Next, you must let go of any judgment as to why you have created things you claim you don't want. This can be difficult because people are taught to attach themselves to situations, results and people. When we judge, we not only squander the hours, but we energetically attach to the very thing we don't want. We begin to see ourselves as that very thing. Learn to develop the skill of detaching from those experiences and become the "curious observer" who is objectively looking in at your life. This is a higher level skill and will take some time to develop, but when you can do this on a consistent and regular basis, you become aware that you have stepped into your divine space. Now you understand that absolutely nothing stands in the way of you and your desires. In this space, there are no such things as obstacles, and you don't have to try and figure out "HOW" you're going to move from your current place to the desired outcome.

Did you know that this is the ONLY PLACE where we can come in contact with Truth? This is also the only place from which we can create our Divine Intention (or manifest our goals and heart's passions). This is the place where we make Quantum Leaps! Simply put, life becomes magical...

Many years ago, I set out on a journey to figure out how people achieved what they wanted in life. I, like many of you, was taught the power of affirmations. I spent years trying to reprogram my subconscious mind through constant and spaced repetition or emotional impact. But deep down I always wondered why this was necessary. If at a soul level we are perfect - we are God - then why do we need all of these silly tools to help us achieve our purpose and complete our life's mission?

If you want to pick up the pace and be on the fast track to goal reaching, then learn to keep it simple. Just listen...there is a serene voice inside of you. One that is attempting to tell you what you really desire in life. You don't need to spend hours shouting out affirmations for your aspirations to come in to fruition. You just need to follow the still, quiet voice inside of you. Just follow the nudges. Jumping through all those affirmation hoops is unnecessary. WHAT A RELIEF!

As you follow that voice, it naturally leads you to a place of "Instant Creation." You become one with the Divine side of yourself. The painful separation between you and your desires that was created by other people's limiting beliefs vanishes. You realize anything you desire is at your command. Your life takes on new meaning.

When you awaken and become conscious of your manifesting capabilities, you realize that the Divine has NO limits and any limit you may perceive is self-imposed. So how do you know when you are in the place of Conscious Manifestation? What are the signs that you've arrived? Ultimately, you become aware of two simple things:

1. You are at Peace (with yourself and the world about you)
2. You Create the Actual Result (your goal, passion or desire has already been achieved)

If you are not manifesting what you want, the problem is not on some outside situation, person or source – the trouble is always you. If you experience only one of the two without the other, then you know you are not in this sacred space. For instance, if you have peace and no result, then you are hiding behind spirituality. You think you're at peace, but you're really not. The truth is, you have created an emotion that mimics peace, but it was created by the false self, the pain self, the ego self. Many people hide in that place for years. Some have dropped their other addictions in life only to pick up and hide behind a new one called spirituality, God or religion. You might find that statement shocking, but it's true! To hide behind these things is just as damaging and unhealthy as any other addiction.

What about the people that reach a goal, but they're miserable? What about the millionaire that has plenty of money in the bank, but is dying inside? Unfortunately, I've worked with many women who have the idea that in order to reach their financial goals, then they must sacrifice their lives with their chosen partners and children. Suffering from the internal turmoil that guilt and frustration brings, they are far from any true form of peace or serenity. They don't understand that they can have both! If you relate to this on any level, then you're not in the sacred space. You MUST have both true peace and the desired result AT THE SAME TIME.

Remember, a great master once said, "the truth will set you free." If you're not free – if you're frustrated because you haven't achieved your dreams – then you're not in your truth. You still lack the knowledge of how powerful you truly are. Not only will you never experience genuine peace and serenity, but you'll also never gain the satisfaction of living your passions and reaching your goals. Sadly, most people on this planet die with deep regrets and without fulfilling their mission in life.

Now, if you are willing to trust in the unseen and step into this place of truth, you will discover the "Kingdom Within," the "Straight Gate," the "Gap" or any other metaphorical explanation used to describe how you experience your true self, God.

Here there are no "how-to" guides. There are no limits. Imagine a world where everything you desire comes to life. You have the ability to create your world. It's a place where your dreams *really* do come true. And it's all yours when you make the decision to remaining open and willing. Stay in the now, trust in the unseen, listen to the quiet voice that echoes in the depths of you, follow your heart and continue to reveal your own power to yourself.

"Just Believe."

David

From high school drop-out to million dollar business owner, David Neagle, Million Dollar Income Acceleration Coach, has mentored thousands of entrepreneurs to achieve levels of success far beyond what they previously thought possible. David currently has clients in 8 countries who regularly travel across the globe to attend his renowned **Experience The Reality of Success** *seminars. David invites you to download his Free 4-hour audio program and accompanying study guide entitled* **The Art of Success** *at www. DavidNeagle.com/artsuccess.html.*

CHAPTER 10

Listening for Signals from Spirit — 5 Tips to Discover Your Self & Your Success

Cornelia Powell

Your life story, with the unique angle of vision it offers, is rich with divine direction. The *signals from Spirit* that you're always receiving not only inspire your inner growth and self-discovery, but when you really tune in, they also act as conscious stepping stones guiding your entrepreneurial vision. Are you hearing your *signals*?

I'm sharing a few stories—and signals!—from my life, to provide insights into deciphering the roadmap of your entrepreneurial journey….and perhaps illuminating some of your stepping stones.

1. Proceed Fearlessly

"Proceed fearlessly," Katharine instructed. Actually it was more like she beamed the words to me as she held my shoulders firmly between her hands, snapping me to attention. Looking squarely into my eyes—with her twinkling, wise-woman gaze—I couldn't escape the power of the moment.

Katharine's voice is strong and full of purpose, but with something like a gurgling chuckle underneath it, so you feel her wisdom backed up with a reminder to "keep it light"!

This is how I received my entrepreneurial marching orders. "Proceed fearlessly" was my directional beam of light to follow into the dazzlingly *"vast unknown"* territory of starting a business.

Katharine and I were teammates in a seminar for *est* training graduates in the early 1980's. My seminar project was to design a new business and organize the "tools" needed to fulfill that vision.

In my participation in the *est* training (which birthed The Landmark Forum), I found a powerful language that enhanced my intuitive nature. I learned that this "Say what you mean and mean what you say" language gives your wishes *power*; your dreams *vision*; your words *purpose*; your inspiration *direction*; your ideas *structure*; and even gives your fears *possibility*. (i.e. How to use everything as a *signal from Spirit*!)

Katharine's instruction, *proceed fearlessly*, did not mean that I would be *without* fear (I was "shaking in my boots" half the time when I first opened my retail business). It was a cue to redirect my attention and not give my fears any power.

The message of *proceed fearlessly* is to encourage you to put attention on what lights you up about your life. Then it's not so easy to become distracted by any bump-in-the-road circumstances and lose sight of what you hold dear. It's a call to stay "awake" so when your fears do pop up, you can thank them for being messengers sent to remind you that it's time to "tend to the fires" of your entrepreneurial vision.

2. Hear *No* as an Opportunity

3. Don't Take Anything *Personally*

I opened an innovative retail store in the mid '80s, a project supported not only by Katharine's fearless nudging, but by other empowering coaches as well (a mainstay for all entrepreneurs!) My shop was an elegant haven for romantics everywhere, especially for "grown-up brides" who had few shopping resources and even less emotional support in that era's "cookie-cutter" wedding world.

Although I created an intimate, rather transformational experience for my customers, developing close relationships with many of them, I learned that it was important for me to distinguish *business* from *personal*. These two tips kept things light and flexible (and may have kept me in business as well!):

- Hear *no* as an opportunity.
- Don't take anything *personally*.

I found that if you stay open and curious, then instead of hearing "no" as some sort of closed door, you hear "no" with a sense of gratitude and can use it as a guide to *what's next*. And even though this is *your* business, if you make it *personal*—such as thinking someone's "no" was "no" to you personally instead of some merchandise, time, or budget related decision—then you give away your power. As one of my coaches advised, "Hear complaints as a direction, not a derailment!"

Following these two mantras was key for me in not only creating a business I loved, but being able to love the process of building a business. And they continue to support keeping a sense of flow and ease to life.

4. Practice Everyday

You know those "deep knowing" kind of '*aha*' moments that come with such certainty that you're clear *it* is going to happen no matter how obscure, strange, or insurmountable it might seem? (Unless, of course, you allow the old fear monster to gobble it up, denying your very soul.)

One of those *signals from Spirit*—to "write a book"—came to me when I had my retail store, even though I was not a writer. (Not just "not a writer," but I resisted writing to the extent that I didn't even make grocery lists!) But as soon as I "heard" the message, I was sure that I would write a book of the stories I shared with brides and their families, opening them to the heart-centered wisdom of their various rites-of-passage.

I love the way of Spirit! Not only did I start writing, but had a *passion* to write when I returned from a trip to China in 2000, a couple of years after closing my store. My experiences into the heart of this ancient and mystical Taoist world were such a spiritual "break open" that I immediately began writing the stories of my journey, including meeting my teacher's teacher who was 128 years old.

Revered as a noble treasure, Grand Master Li Cheng Yu and the priestesses who cared for her, welcomed our group into their tiny, modest home—in a thousand-year-old burnt-out temple compound. Her former student, my teacher Master Chen, interpreted as the elder sage thanked us for coming to visit; asked for our support in assisting her "new" project of rebuilding the temple; and reminded us to "take care of the children."

She punctuated each message in her lyrical singsong voice with, "and don't forget, practice everyday." Then as we were leaving, Grand Master Li, regally sitting in her lotus position just as she had received us, began doing Tai Chi. I wept at the beauty and power of this image; not only moved by the devotion to her practice, but the devoted practice that was her life.

If she can "practice everyday" for 128 years, then surely I can as well! And not just the meditative, healing Qi Gong movements of her lineage, but practice doing all the things I loved, that lit me up, that connected me deeply with Spirit and the purpose of my life.

And I began writing *that* book as soon as I returned home! The practice of "building a book" became a crucial component in my future entrepreneurial ventures. Fearlessly following those "deep knowing" messages into what seems like the *vast unknown* usually means that you're on the right track.

The everyday practice of tuning in to your heart-center feeds your mind, body and soul, revealing your purpose, and is the link to fine-tuning your *signals from Spirit.*

5. Open Your Heart

"You have heart, Cornelia. We need you here," one of the senior editors at *Vogue* magazine told me. I had ventured to New York City—following one of those *spirit signals*—at the age of 22, ripe off my family's Alabama farm.

In those years in the early 1970's, I got to explore "the other side of the mountain" and the magic learned from "strangers," honing skills and talents that may never have been called forth under less demanding circumstances.

Having some mileage in the territory of the *vast unknown*—this time by the name of New York City!—was helpful years later, not only when I began my entrepreneurial journey, but also my journey into the mysteries of meditation, where the "you have heart" message revealed its secret.

My practice of *Tai Chi*, then *Qi Gong*, lead me to study meditation, first in the ancient discipline of the Taoist (which was tough for a lazy "meditator" like me), then I was introduced to a fast and effective, spirit-guided modern "technique." *Living at Ease* is an easy, fun program that quiets your mind, "drops" you into the still wisdom of your body, opens the doorway to your Spirit, then gives you the "return address" of this sweet place of stillness and ease.

You can live there as your permanent address as long as you *practice*: practice noticing subtle things; practice putting attention on what lights you up; practice *opening your heart* and connecting with people from this intimate, more aware place of being.

This practice guided me when I began a new entrepreneurial adventure in 2006. I discovered that the *mysteries into the void* of stillness and meditation became comforting and empowering "business partners." And something to consider: Isn't running a business while intentionally *keeping your heart open* the genuine nature of a true "partnership"?

Perhaps all *signals from Spirit* are the same message: "Open your heart and practice keeping it open." I invite you to engage in this practice. Possibly it's the key to you not only being a *conscious entrepreneur*, but being a true success as one.

During her 30 years as an entrepreneur, Cornelia has worked with thousands of women—brides, their mothers, grandmothers, sisters, friends—and tells their stories that speak to the hearts of all women in her online magazine, **Weddings of Grace** *(www.WeddingsOfGrace.com). Her blog,* **The Woman You Become** *(www.WomanYouBecome.com), shares messages*

of "women becoming" all that their hearts' desire. Please join her for a bit of connection and delight—and **free gifts!** She'd love to hear your story. Cornelia@CorneliaPowell.com.

CHAPTER 11

Heaven School—
How to Create Heaven Inside and Out

Michele Risa

What if you could hop a plane, enter Heaven, and enroll in a school where you obtained insights that would dramatically improve the quality of your life?

Even better, what if these insights were always available to you . . . easily accessible in your day-to-day life?

Best of all, what if you were able to create heavenly peace inside your body and out? Like a master, you would feel and radiate calm despite the surrounding chaos.

That's what "Heaven" School offers.

Similar to the ancient schools of Egypt, Greece, India and China, Heaven School offers lessons and insights normally unavailable in more traditional settings.

All this translates into living a conscious life and being a conscious entrepreneur.

The Benefits to Living Consciously

The benefits of living consciously are a thousand fold. You make your life a great story - a love story - because someone always loves you. You feel wonderful because you treat yourself with kindness, compassion, and forgiveness. You generate an attitude of gratitude which attracts more to be grateful for. You create your life as opposed to reacting to it, turning old, unhealthy habits into new opportunities. People come to learn from you, thereby increasing your stature and influence, and together create new possibilities for the human family.

Where You Begin

It all begins with you -- the source. The climate of your interior world determines how you respond and what kind of life you create.

Some examples: What if your boss asks you to solve a problem? Can you best leave a good impression for future situations when you're exhausted or well rested? Or if at a party, would you more likely attract someone if you feel unsure or exuberant?

So the $64,000 question is: How do you CHOOSE who you want to be?

The answer is not written in the stars, but in your heart. In every moment you actually decide your life . . . either consciously or unconsciously.

What the Unconscious Life Sounds Like

When living unconsciously, your habits run most of your life. On automatic pilot for so long, you barely know what causes your undesired outcomes. Even when someone offers constructive feedback, it is difficult to change your behavior because you're caught in your old way of believing, feeling, thinking, and seeing.

You're hearing (and creating) a constant chatter in your mind that goes on every minute of every day. It can sound like this: "Life's not fair." Everyone my age is overweight." "I'll never have a lot of money." "Smoking is too hard a habit to break." "There are no decent men left." "I knew it wasn't going to work." What can you expect from these habitual assumptions, expectations and negative affirmations?

Language creates the reality it describes.

Often, we talk about where we want to go, but lack the necessary tools, processes or maps to get there.

Tools That Truly Support a Conscious Life

At Heaven School, that's what you get. You begin to replace old reactions with responses that truly support you and allow you to live every moment consciously. Here is a sample of tools and phrases that can help:

- You Don't Know What You Don't Know
- You Are Not Your Thoughts
- Your Comfort Zone Can Create Conflict and Cost You Your Peace
- How To Create Calm Amid The Chaos
- The Feelings You've Denied, Ignored, and Suppressed Can Heal Your Heart
- Relationships Are Mirrors
- You Are Already Using The Law of Attraction
- An Attitude of Gratitude Will Change Your Life
- The New Definition of Perfection Includes Mistakes, Darkness and Death

Knowing is the first step but it is not enough. You must *experience* it for yourself. You must bring it into your life and make it your own.

Try this great exercise I once heard from author/coach Rebbie Straubing:

Imagine you are pregnant. (Men, this may present a bigger hurdle for you.) You are carrying a special baby...YOU. Everything you feel, think, and eat affects your fetus. Each moment, the environment in your womb determines your growth and well-being. Close your eyes and commit right now to love and nourish yourself- however you define that- for the next nine months. See what you deliver!

Granted, it's hard to do. We've all tried many times in one way or another to love and cherish ourselves.

Who hasn't wished instead for a magic wand to quickly reach our dreams of wealth, health, and love? Yet reaching the final goal DOES NOT provide a life filled with happiness and success. As you know, once you make $100,000 you want $200,000. Still, we grasp for the gold ring and despair at coming up empty handed.

Reaching Your Goal Is Less Important Than You May Think

That's because the real "gem" is acquired by going through the process or taking the journey. As my teacher, Yogi Bhajan taught, "You must begin the journey - a journey just 12 inches long - from your mind to your heart."

Like a diamond, the pressure and polishing along life's way makes us shine! You get to practice being courageous, committed, compassionate, and forgiving. You learn to be authentic, speak your truth, say no without guilt, and say yes and mean it.

How to Use Your Feelings to Your Advantage

Your feelings are powerful. Here's how to use them positively. You're having a stressful day so decide to take a break. Someone offers you a yummy chocolate cookie. You think, "This will make me feel good." But what if having long-lasting energy, a healthy weight, or reducing your chances of diabetes or heart attack makes you feel even better? Which would you choose?

When living a joyful life feels the best, you don't want to choose anything else. The bottom line? To make what is ACTUALLY good for you, feel good.

A quick tip: If you want to feel confident about new goals, first feel good about what you've already accomplished. This makes you feel empowered about what you can achieve now.

The more you practice using these new tools, the more skilled you'll become, the more automatic the new behavior will get, and the easier your life will be. Like learning to play the piano, practice is the key to creating change in your life.

Being The "Lone Ranger" Is Out… Joining Community Is In

You have your tools at hand and you're passionate about practicing them. You try it on your own, but it's harder than expected. Happily, the time of the "Lone Ranger" is over. At Heaven School you're connected to a community.

Research has proven that having support is critical to success. It helps you to maintain momentum and see obstacles as nothing more than something to get around or over, not as the time to give up. It helps you see that success is not about failure, but failing and getting back up.

The community helps you harness your strength and the resolve to be unstoppable.

You also get the rare opportunity to be surrounded with giving, receiving, and gratitude. It's a special place to practice forgiveness, the cornerstone for healing and peace.

At Heaven School you celebrate your body. You cultivate sensitivity to energy to achieve a sense of completeness and balance within yourself. You learn to connect to your breath, strengthen your nervous system, activate your glandular system, balance your emotional energies, and channel your mind to access your intuitive awareness.

In this way, your energy will be available to attract what you need and allow you to make your unique contribution to the world.

You Can't Help But Make a Difference

Being a conscious entrepreneur enables you to right the wrongs of the world... to join the ranks of Bill Gates and Warren Buffett. Being a conscious entrepreneur allows you to choose: To live your dreams or nightmares, to foster forgiveness or revenge in our culture, and to promote heavenly creation or hellish destruction in the world.

So who better than this conscious human to create heaven on earth? A conscious human who truly recognizes there is more than enough to go around. Enough money and enough power for everyone, so that 'win-win' becomes the universal solution and not just a catchy phrase.

It's time for the new trilogy -- self, community and the universe -- where old boundaries no longer apply. Not at the individual level, the national level, or even the ends of the universe.

But where to start? Once again, with the source -- you. You have been blessed with so much that it can't help but spill out to everyone and everything in your life. And the fact that we're all connected energetically, despite our physical separation, allows us the opportunity to impact each other as well as truly love all humans as family.

You create your life every single moment of every day. Why not create the life you really want and have fun doing it, while living a life that inspires you and the world?

Join us at Heaven School . . . a little "peace" of bliss on earth.

Michele Risa knows about the journey. As a lifelong explorer, she's intimately connected with living consciously. A TV producer of her yoga show since 1998, she's also a motivational speaker who has trained with the "masters," stirring audiences by sharing her understanding of life's complexities and its great lessons. Authentic to the core, she's run marathons and traveled the world in pursuit of living more deeply. Come create new possibilities and receive a free, inspiring audio at www.BeyondBodyMindSpirit.com.

CHAPTER 12

Adventures in Entrepreneurship

Geanine Thompson

I'm convinced that the craziest thing you could ever do in this life is to become an entrepreneur. Your family and friends will wonder why you insist on being different and difficult. They'll ponder why you refuse to do what everyone else is doing and won't get a "real" job. They want you to stop playing around, settle down and 'get with the program.' Besides, it's for your own good, you know. They know what's best for you since you obviously don't.

I know you don't want to hear this, but to some degree they're right. You might be a tad crazy, but don't let that get you down. That's exactly what you need to survive this adventure.

In my case, I started out working for Fortune 500 financial services firms and worked my way up to Senior Vice President of Marketing for a premier wealth management firm. Although I loved marketing financial services, I discovered that I also enjoyed the autonomy and variation of consulting assignments, and subsequently built a career as a successful Marketing Consultant.

In an effort to generate fresh business ideas, I attended a marketing conference for solo entrepreneurs and learned about a host of new marketing and operating business models and strategies. I didn't know it then, but by the final day of the conference, the trajectory of my life had been changed forever. My week-long experience at the conference served as a catalyst; it fueled my dormant sense of adventure and helped me figure out how to combine my passion for education, specifically my college admissions counseling experience, with my marketing expertise.

Several months later, my new business was born -- The College Guru™, a college admissions counseling firm that organizes, prioritizes and guides parents and students through the ultra competitive college application process. Each day is an adventure as I take on the multifaceted role of chief strategist, drill sergeant and cheerleader for students trying to find their place at a selective college.

Now what about you? No matter where you are in your entrepreneurial journey, the idea formation stage, new business owner or seasoned veteran, there are some tenants that hold true for those of us who are taking the road less traveled. On days when you are overwhelmed and unclear about what to do next, consider the ideas here to help get you back on the right track!

Be authentic

This is not so easy to do given we are bombarded with celebrity images that serve to illustrate and reinforce that our original selves are not good enough. Don't fall for it! Be brave enough to be you. You may be soft spoken or more of a bull-in-the-china-shop personality, but it really doesn't matter. Just stand up and share the real you, quirks and all, then watch people take notice. No, don't wait until you get an extreme makeover or lose those last stubborn 10 pounds. Show up and be yourself fully without apology. Share your unique gifts. Who you are right now is good enough.

Live your life purpose

When I identified my life purpose it frightened me. Was it true that I'm here for a reason? Do I have what it takes to be that person? Will I have the courage to define my business as an extension of that purpose and do what I was born to do? What will people think of me? After a lot of reflection, I decided it was important to do what was best for me. I've since taken the stance that I am reflected in my business, and my business is an expression of me. I encourage you to take the time to define and consider your life purpose, what you are here to do and then do it.

Implement your plan

If you can't recall anything else from my chapter, please remember this: Implement, implement, implement! Successful businesses act on their ideas and unsuccessful businesses do not. We live in a time of 'analysis paralysis.' I've been guilty of it myself what with my large corporation roots. I've attended meetings about meetings, and know how easy it is to fall in love with your plan. You've spent lots of time thinking great thoughts and had the courage to put them on paper. Plans are invaluable as they provide direction and vision. However, there comes a time when you have to put down the paper and do something, take action. Remember that if you choose not to act, you will not have customers. And without customers, you will not have a business. No matter how scary it is, get out there and get it done.

Ignore criticism

Once your family and friends realize what you're doing, they're going to have ideas about your business - lots of them. Unless they are your target market or fellow entrepreneurs, respectfully ignore them. Love them, but do not let them drive your business plan. No matter how much they love you, they will not understand. For example, one day I was hard at work fine-tuning my product offerings and shared this information with a friend. Although for years I'd been paid handsomely to develop products and services for major financial services firms, her encouraging response was, "Do you know how to do that?" Enough said.

Be courageous and persevere

It takes courage to go on your own and create something from nothing, not to mention the financial risk inherent in these decisions. The best advice I can give you is to stay in action. Some days you'll accomplish a lot, other days not as much, but keep moving. I'm always amazed that if I stay in action, in a relatively short period of time, I'll have a trail of accomplishments behind me! I'm learning to be more patient with myself and to know that I don't have to do it all right now, this very second, or the world as we know it will cease to exist. And on those days when you're overwhelmed, I encourage you to let out a primal scream, cry for a few minutes or chow down on Haagen-Dazs and then get back to work.

Accept that you will make mistakes

Leave perfection at the door. As a recovering perfectionist, I know how hard this is. I'm one of those people who used to worship at the altar of perfection and I am here to tell you, it's a false god. I pride myself on a job exceedingly well done just like the next person, however, I've learned that it's more important to get the product or service out the door. I used to scoff at an entrepreneur who would do things like schedule a major conference before completing the presentation. The conversation in my head would go something like, "Is she crazy? That's just not done! Doesn't she know there is a proper way to do things?" Yet as I started to observe how much she accomplished and how much money she made (after all, part of this is about the money), I realized that maybe I had it all wrong. Now I get things to a good state and then let them out into the world. I no longer second guess myself and shoot down the idea without giving it a chance to either succeed or fail. If the idea doesn't work, I tweak it or abort the mission and try something else. You and your business will continue to evolve and that means you will make mistakes.

Have fun

Enjoy the process as well as your success. I continue to work on this one as I'm notorious for starting a project, watching it take root and then running off to the next big thing. Now I take the time to acknowledge and congratulate myself. I tell myself that I am absolutely fabulous (this takes practice) and then share my triumphs with my entrepreneur friends. In addition, I try not to take myself so seriously. I must confess this did not come easily to me after spending many years working on Wall Street.

Remember: This is *your* business. Embrace it. Own it. Enjoy it. Live and love your life!

"Just be yourself and say what you feel because those who mind don't matter and those who matter don't mind."

~ DR. SEUSS

Geanine Thompson is Founder and CEO of The College Guru™, a college admissions counseling firm. A graduate of Dartmouth College with a BA in English, she continued her studies at Duke University, the Fuqua School of Business where she received an MBA. She has extensive experience developing marketing strategies for Fortune 500 financial services firms in her roles as Senior Vice President and Marketing Consultant. For FREE tips on winning college admissions strategies go to www.TheCollegeGuru.com.

CHAPTER 13

The "Kei" to a Thriving Business

Dallas Travers, CEC

After more than six years as the president of my own company, I've learned a lot about what it takes to create a thriving business. I've learned how to manage budgets, train personnel, sell effectively, and invest wisely. The most valuable lesson I've learned has nothing to do with the numbers, the staff, or the nuts and bolts of business activity. Instead, it simply involves the power of perspective.

In Chinese, the word crisis is composed of two characters. One character (Wei) represents danger and the other (Kei) represents opportunity. A crisis is a turning point or a pivotal moment in time. Entrepreneurs face these turning points daily, especially during the start-up phases of the company. When operating your business, do you choose danger or do you choose opportunity?

My good friend Sean loves to play poker. He participates in tournaments regularly and loves studying the game as well as its players, many of whom play professionally. Sean believes that there are two kinds of poker players: the ones who play to win and the ones who play to not lose. Those who play to win, focus more on opportunity. They are committed to learning, improving, and winning big. They understand that part of winning big means losing at times. They even treat their losses as learning opportunities that will translate into future wins. The poker players who play to not lose seem to be so afraid they will run out of chips that their primary focus becomes about avoiding zero. Distracted by their fear of losing, these players rarely win in the end. When your only goal is hanging on to one chip, you'll most likely end up with just one chip.

Winning poker players trust their instincts, design a strategy, embrace bold decisions, and ultimately take home the big bucks because of it. The same is possible in business when you maintain a Kei perspective.

Focusing on opportunity offers endless possibility. By embracing a crisis as an opportunity, you can focus on growth, experience and forward motion. Operating from this place, you can clearly distinguish fact from fiction.

Conversely, focusing on danger or fear, your primary concern becomes about survival - the danger controls you. Fear motivates you to avoid harm and to simply get by. When operating from a danger-consciousness, your options are limited to those alternatives connected to the fear itself, which in turn only create more fear. Your actions become motivated by emotions or ideas about what might happen rather than what is actually true. This leaves you stuck in a state of contemplation or avoidance, preventing you from taking positive action.

Author and philosopher, Florence Scovel Shinn once wrote, "Nothing but fear and doubt stands between a man and his highest ideals and every desire of his heart. When a man can wish without worrying, every desire will be instantly fulfilled. We must substitute faith for fear, for fear is only inverted faith; it is faith in evil instead of good."

My business turned around overnight when I moved away from fear and into faith. I started my own company at the ripe-old-age of 24. I secured a business loan, created a business plan and set up shop over a period of about 30 days. For the first two years in business, fear was calling all of the shots. My fear of failure paralyzed me. Afraid of not having enough money, I worried everyday about money. I avoided investing in the business in order to hang on to what little money I had. Afraid of being judged or rejected, I avoided advertising and spreading the word about the service I provided. Afraid of overcharging, I offered services at a significantly lower rate or even for free. By charging these low rates, I was essentially telling my clients that I did not value my own business and they in turn did not value the service I provided.

My fear of failure paralyzed me and prevented me from taking any action. When I focused on failure, rejection, or lack of resources, all of my decisions originated from those fearful places. As a result, my business didn't grow, I couldn't pay the rent, and I was miserable.

I continued to struggle and worry, but eventually grew tired of being afraid. I realized that if my business was going to survive, I had to change my perspective. With nothing to lose, I decided to try an experiment. For thirty days, I ignored my problems and fears and only focused on positive possibilities. I decided to switch from fear to faith (which I later came to understand to be choosing a Kei rather than a Wei perspective). I rejected all fear-based thoughts and operated my current business as though it already was successful, thriving, and expanding every day. I took risks. I played to win.

Immediately, new and exciting opportunities presented themselves. I said yes to every opportunity. Then I took action with the faith that my business would benefit, and it did. I doubled my client base and doubled my income in less than thirty days. My company has grown more than I ever expected since I replaced fear with faith and embraced a Kei perspective. Now, I confidently take risks, commit to learning every day, and enjoy helping my clients achieve their greatest goals. With a Kei perspective, I no longer allow a fear of failure to overshadow my potential and the possibilities for my business.

I eliminated my fears by focusing on my love for my clients, my passion for the service I provided, and my faith in the opportunities ahead of me. These values meant more to me than any perceived fears I felt, and by focusing on these values, the Wei seemed no longer an option.

Making the shift

Shifting from a fear-based Wei perspective to a passionate Kei perspective involves three steps.

Step One: Identify what values or commitments matter most to you and to your business. What motivates you? How would you like your work to impact your world and the world around you?

You may value education or service to others. You may value money, freedom, adventure, philanthropy, or personal growth. As an entrepreneur, your commitments might include success or achievement, contributing to your community, or excelling in the marketplace. It's important to identify what matters most to you and your business so that you can hold those values in mind when making crucial decisions.

Step Two: Set your fears aside. They may feel very real, but focusing on them does not serve your business. Focus on your values and commitments, and identify what you value most. What is possible? What opportunities do your commitments present? Brainstorm with others as often as you can and see what new opportunities arise.

If you value freedom and flexibility most, you may realize that the best way to expand your business is to align yourself with other synergistic businesses, so that you can rely on others to spread the word about what you do. If you value education and personal growth, perhaps you will see how investing in continued education will allow you to take your business to the next level.

Step Three: Focus only on these opportunities. Write them down and read them daily. What action can you take to step into a Kei perspective? Do not worry about developing the perfect plan. Just take consistent action and trust in your values.

By setting your fears aside, identifying your core values, and taking consistent action, you cannot lose with a Kei perspective. You will notice that by utilizing your values and commitments to seize opportunities, fears immediately dissipate. Replace your fears with your passions and watch the opportunities unfold.

Dallas Travers is the president and founder of Sage Creative Inc., an innovative consulting company for actors, artists and other creative professionals. A certified Creative Career Coach, Dallas infuses practical knowledge with inspired ideas that motivate entrepreneurs to blaze bold paths and positively impact the lives of others. To download your free Values Appraisal or to learn more about Dallas, please visit www.dallastravers.com.

CHAPTER 14

What do *you* choose to "Be a Stand For"?

Jan Wehner

"As Ye Sow, So Shall Ye Reap"

Some form of these words flow throughout human history and all spiritual texts. These words reflect a universal truth that your thoughts, words and actions are returned to you 'in kind.' It is essential to choose what you want to 'reap' in all areas of your life, and then to 'sow' the seeds through your words and deeds.

"When one bases his life on principle, 99 percent of his decisions are already made."

~ AUTHOR UNKNOWN

Your Business

Congratulations! You have made two important decisions.

First, you have chosen the path of the entrepreneur - to offer your products or services into the world, to give value to others and to gain worth for yourself through financial rewards.

Second, you have chosen to read this book and this article about Conscious Business. As you will have learned by now, Conscious Business means making choices which ensure that your interactions in the marketplace and in your personal life make a positive difference in the world. You will also have learned that to own a Conscious Business is to create a *successful business* – built on a solid foundation to stand the tests of time.

Many other entrepreneurs are in such a hurry to reach their success goals that they go to any lengths to do it. They risk making hasty decisions that seem to be solid at the time, but which have hidden costs. Some of these costs may take the form of backlash from those whose toes they step on in their rush up the success ladder.

You are probably aware of the phrase "One bad apple spoils the barrel." Poor decisions and the actions that arise from them create unhappy relationships and ill will – or 'bad apples.' It only takes a handful of unhappy people to turn the tide of interest away from you and your enterprise – and it takes a lot more effort and energy to regain ground lost through a poor reputation than it does to create a good reputation in the first place.

There is Another Way

By making careful decisions today with an eye focused on the long term, a Conscious Entrepreneur will create a path of goodwill that will lead to greater benefit in the long run. This entrepreneur will have a set of guidelines or values that will be used to weigh out the merits of a particular decision, in both short and long term results.

How do you arrive at your own set of guidelines and values? By determining what your foundational or core beliefs are. Perhaps you most cherish honesty, integrity, giving greater value than you receive back, preserving or healing the environment, being of service, or any of a number of other worthy values.

A phrase that I have come to appreciate lately is to 'Be a Stand For' something that I value. For me, this means a deep, life-shaping declaration about what I care about and what I will take action on and it arises from my deepest desire for what I want for the world as a whole. This is a position of leadership that is inclusive and proactive, and is empowering of others – a solid foundation for building a life of meaning and contribution *and* a financially successful business.

One way to determine what you 'Stand For' would be to undertake an exercise to note what you 'Do Not Like' in your dealings with and knowledge of other businesses or relationships. Then, note the contrasting qualities that you 'Do or Would Value' in a business or relationship. This will help you to determine your core values.

Next, expand on these values to lay out the particular actions you will take to implement them in your business. You can then craft your Vision (what your business looks like as it successfully carries out its purpose) and Mission (the purpose for your business to exist) statements for your business enterprise to reflect these core values.

Your core values, Vision and Mission statements, and the 'Stand For' you choose to be will then permeate your life, and will animate every conversation and action in your business and influence every decision you make. They will become the cornerstones of your business plan, your marketing strategy and will determine the actions which arise from them.

These decisions and actions will honor the integrity of the relationship with all parties in the business transaction:

* potential customers, partners or colleagues
* competitors
* yourself

Let's look at these in greater detail.

Potential Customers, Partners or Colleagues

It is important to spend time understanding your values in order to determine your purpose for contacting potential customers, partners or colleagues, *before* you develop your marketing plan and do any advertising. Are you just looking for a quick sale or are you hoping to develop a long-term relationship with these people if the interaction is successful? The approach will be very different depending on your answer.

If you are looking for a one-time quick sale, or are not concerned about longevity in your business, you might engage in overstatement or evasion in your marketing. You certainly don't expect to be around when a negative reaction ensues. You would not, obviously, be practicing Conscious Business principles.

If you are looking to build a long-term relationship, then declaring your values in some way in your advertising, website, and conversations will help your 'prospects' (and you) to determine whether you have compatible values as a foundation to build upon. You can do this directly through stating your values, or through the language you use in writing your ad copy, website text and, of course, direct conversations.

Your clear values will also allow you to 'keep the door open' with those who don't choose to join your enterprise just now. This is important because they may make another choice in the future when their circumstances change. They might also refer their contacts to you based on the 'positive feelings' they retain from their interaction with you.

Competitors

You may wonder at the necessity of being considerate of your competitors, but it is a very significant concern. As the world 'grows smaller' through the interconnectivity of the Internet and global news media, people are more aware of the pattern of unethical behavior that has tarnished the reputation of many businesses and individuals in the past few years.

There are methods of marketing available now that take advantage of the success of others. For instance, by 'ambushing' their prospects and placing your website in front of theirs while they pay the advertising costs. These approaches put your business forward at the expense of others, rather than based on its own merit and your own efforts.

Another questionable practice is the use of negative advertising – such as promoting your business by criticizing another one. Most people will see through that approach and will wonder why – if the advertiser's company or product is worth considering – they need to promote it by putting another one down.

The real problem with these kinds of advertising is that it makes the whole marketing community look like 'kids in a sandlot' calling each other names. It cheapens everyone's business and makes people shy away from trusting that anyone is truthful and fair.

While some people will not have qualms about these kinds of negative ads, or be bothered that your ad 'popped up' over something they had chosen to view, others are quite upset by the feeling of being manipulated. The short-term gains carry hidden costs in terms of your reputation and the image you are presenting for your business.

The tide is turning toward holding businesses – and their representatives – accountable for their ethics and actions. You don't want to invite 'negative reviews' based on your negative advertising methods.

Yourself

This is actually the most important consideration because integrity is the foundation on which your *life* is built – not just your business. If your core values are based on ethical action, honesty, spirituality, fairness, contributing value to the world, compassion, or any number of others, you will want to conduct yourself in a way that supports these values.

It is much simpler to live a life consistent with your values in every area. Anyone who has 'told a little lie' in order to gain something, knows how tricky it can be to maintain and to contain the lie. Having a central pillar of values, and 'Being A Stand For' those values takes the guesswork out of every decision. You just 'know' what to do without having to 'figure it out.'

How to Be a 'Magnet' in Your Marketing

One great way to promote yourself and your offering with a magnetic energy is to 'move toward the positive.' Express the benefits of your offer without putting down or pushing against any other option (except, perhaps, the option of taking no action). People will be drawn to your clear, positive, helpful energy and to the leadership you are showing in offering solutions to their problems.

Building your business through making quality decisions and giving full value always – even if it seems slower at first – is the only way to build a solid business, quality relationships, and to give value into the world. What are *you* a 'Stand For'?

Jan Wehner is a writer, speaker, and ethical business owner. Jan 'Is a Stand For' choosing personal responsibility and creating life-by-choice-and-design through attitudes and actions. She inspires others to develop their own businesses to add value to the world. Her mission is 'to be a catalyst for 1,000,000 people to take action toward their purpose.' You can learn more about her, the business model she follows, and subscribe to her Prosperity and Purpose newsletter by visiting http://www.abundanceofchoice.com.

CHAPTER 15

Creating Conscious Decisions with Certainty

Vanessa Wesley

Wouldn't it be fabulous if you had a trusted advisor who knew exactly the right decisions to make - one you could consult anytime you wanted to . . . for free?

Imagine there was a way to know, with certainty, what decisions to make.

Imagine you had an inner compass that pointed true to *your* north, and not to someone else's.

Perhaps you're already aware that an inner guidance system, a kind of inner advisor or compass exists. You may call it instinct, or intuition. You know it's there, but you don't recognize, trust, or know how to follow it unconditionally. What has it cost you in time, money, or even cherished dreams, to go in one direction while your compass pointed in another? What would your 'to do' list look like, or your strategic business plans, or your priorities and commitments if you knew with certainty what to put your attention, focus, and energy on?

Recently, I was talking with the producer of a women's radio show about these very questions. She said, "Vanessa, each week I talk to scores of business and professional women who are walking around with a hole in them. A hole? I've never heard it said that way before. A hole—an emptiness—that many are not even aware they have. She called it "a quiet desperation", and it isn't just women who are experiencing this.

The symptoms of this "quiet desperation" are uncomfortably clear. They are feelings of confusion, depression, boredom, and worry. Regrettably, these feelings oftentimes are considered normal—the "way it is" and "business as usual." Yet they are symptoms that our 'internal advisor' was ignored or vetoed.

Good news! There is a way to make decisions with certainty, and I mean *consciously* with *absolute certainty*. Conscious decisions require awareness of the clear, yet subtle sensations that "tell" you 'yes or no', 'go or stop.' These intrinsic (built-in) vibrations are the voice of your wise advisor I call *your essential Whisper*. The sensations of your Whisper are the same for all of us. They are embedded in six types of experiences we've all had.

First, let's take a look at what these sensations are and then I'll cover the six experiences that enable us to recognize them.

The Voice of the Whisper

The "yes" sensations from inner guidance are:

- Peace - abiding wellness
- Presence, high awareness and attentiveness
- Expansion - openness, spaciousness
- Neutrality - detachment to the outcome
- Energy - liveliness toward action
- Certainty and sureness, the sensation of alignment
- Love, deep sense of well-being

Do you know what these sensations feel like in your body? The key to recognizing these is to remember the times in your life when you have experienced them.

Below I have listed the six distinct ways to recognize inner guidance, your essential Whisper. In fact, as you read them you may find yourself exclaiming, "That happened to me!"

So here's what's important. It isn't whether you recognize these experiences, because chances are you will. It's about whether you follow and trust these experiences when they occur in your life, day to day, moment to moment. The truth is we never lost connection to our essential nature of peace and clarity. We never lost our directional signals.

The Six Distinct Experiences

These experiences have characteristics in common. First, they share some, (or all) of the inner sensations listed above, especially Presence. Second, they feel highly significant and meaningful to you. And finally, they occur as distinct experiences that defy explanation, logic, or limitations. As you recall your experiences, see if you can locate the "yes" sensations you felt of certainty, peace, and energy.

Snap-Shot Click

This is a highly significant experience that stands out in your memory like a photograph or frozen scene. Even if the event occurred when you were a child or teen, its image is vivid and clear. Often we forget snapshots until they arise spontaneously when needed, and usually that's when the significance becomes apparent and "clicks."

One story I like to tell is how, when I was eight, a young boy walked into my third grade classroom. I watched him intensely as I found him intriguing. At one point our eyes locked. I became very present in that moment. **Snap**. He left the room, and I completely forgot the incident. In my early twenties I was faced with a marriage decision. Spontaneously, the snapshot flooded my memory filling me with peace and wellness. I realized I already knew the answer. **Click**. I married the man who was the boy.

Collapsed Time

Collapsed Time is when all the "rules" about time seem to have fallen away. It's experienced as an event taking place in slow motion, or alternatively, the experience goes by so fast you lose "track of time." These events of collapsed time feel "timeless", open, and expansive. Pay attention to shifts in your perception of time, as well as the messages you receive.

An endearing man shared how he had plummeted five stories to the ground. He recalled with almost frightening detail the thoughts, actions, and decisions he made while he was falling. The specifics and description he relayed was amazingly vivid for an event that probably took five seconds. What he remembered most was the peace. He said, "I felt eternal."

Urge

Have you ever had a sudden urge to go somewhere, call someone, or do something, and you couldn't figure out why? Then later, the "reason" became apparent, but only after you took action. Take a moment and locate a memory of an urge that you followed through on. Can you recall the energy that rushed in with the urge? What happened? Did the reason for the urge become apparent to you?

Years ago, I had an urge to go to the bookstore. It came on suddenly. I couldn't think of any books I needed, but I went anyway. While there, a man approached me and struck up a conversation. He invited me to be interviewed on his television program. Within a few weeks, I was working with him as an Assistant News Director (even though I had no experience) and became a local celebrity!

I act quickly on the energy of urges from inner guidance. I make decisions based on that energy – no impelling energy, no decision. I've learned to trust it implicitly. You can too!

Wonderment

Wonderment is the state of awe, and delightful amazement. It acts as a direct answer to something you were wondering about, or a heart-felt question you were asking. There you were, just merely thinking about how you were going to get something done and *poof!* - The answer seems to magically appear.

It is typical to become doubtful and uncertain when confronted with a tough decision. You can, however, intentionally invoke Wonderment when you feel uncertain or worried about a decision you're considering. Try this: 1. Write down what you are worried about. 2. Change it to, "I wonder how *this (name your worry)* will happen", or, "I wonder what the best decision will be." 3. Let it go. Surrender to pure potential. Notice what shows up and be amazed!

Knowing

Knowing is the definite and confident impression you get when you "know that you know what you know." You have no clue how you know, yet you feel aligned, assured, and positive pursuing a particular course of action. Knowing may come with an urge to take action, but sometimes you feel Knowing and there is nothing else to do or decide. You simply follow what unfolds.

Inspiration

Inspiration is elevated energy urging you to create. It generally hits you unexpectedly and spontaneously. Suddenly you get an idea filling you with explosive exuberance and motivation. You can't wait to get started. It doesn't matter whether you have experience with, or knowledge of, what you're inspired to create. Sometimes people instilled with inspiration let it fade away because they think they should know the sequence of steps to take. Not true! Inspiration infuses you with energy and information to get started and to take action. The steps are revealed along the way. The "quiet desperation" referred to earlier is often inspiration not acted upon.

Your Conscious Connection

Recalling these six experiences allows you to revive the sensations of peace, Presence, energy, and certainty, making them indelibly recognizable. Doing this leads you to trust the wisdom guiding your actions and choices. As you visit the option and choices of a decision you are facing, ask yourself what sensations arise for each alternative. Does a particular selection bring energy and inspiration, or does it bring fear and doubt? Does working on a specific project feel timeless and energizing, or does it drag?

Familiarize yourself with these sensations and experiences. Recognize and trust them as your compass, your conscious connection to peace and inner wisdom. Enjoy creating, planning, and deciding with absolute certainty.

It's not magical . . . but it certainly feels like it!

Vanessa Wesley has studied and practiced various methodologies in personal growth for over 20 years. She uses a unique system to locate and deactivate stress called Evolutional Kinesiology™. Co-author of **Your Essential Whisper,** *internet radio host, national speaker, and Co-Founder Intrinsic International LLC, she demystifies inner guidance and offers a blueprint for women in personal and business transition to banish self-doubt, and enjoy abundance, self-confidence, and inner peace. Visit www.BodyVoiceTechnologies.com and www.YourEssentialWhisper.com for more information.*

CHAPTER 16

From Busyness to Full Self-Expression: How to Align Your Life (and productivity) with Your Highest Values

Jackie Woodside, LICSW

There is a Cultural Conversation of Busyness.

Have you ever noticed that everyone is too busy? When an experience is pervasive in our midst, it's what sociologists call a "cultural conversation." That's a sophisticated way of saying that an experience is so inherent in our way of life that it has become a "given." It's something that everyone feels and experiences without much, if any, conscious awareness. Creating a life beyond a "cultural conversation" requires awareness and discernment.

This chapter provides a framework to shift from being "busy", to living our lives with ease and grace in alignment with our vision, values and mission.

Your relationship to time

The place to begin is by understanding your current relationship to time. Do you relate to time like it is your ally or your enemy? Most people relate to time from a sense of lack, that is, there's not enough time. This is a distorted view since time is not a variable. How you plan and use your time is the key. No one likes to admit that they're too busy because they're trying to do more in a given day or week than is humanly possible! Ask yourself, "Have I committed to things that would actually require more hours than are in a given day or week?" I've yet to work with someone who said "no" to that question, once they actually sat down and located all of their commitments in time.

There is endless information regarding "time management." Yet, in reality, there is no such thing as managing time – it simply 'is.' What needs to be managed is ourselves (and this is perhaps the "bad news" for many of us!) All you have is time and choice: You can manage your decisions, values, commitments and your priorities, but you cannot manage time. In fact, if you fail to manage yourself, I guarantee someone else will do it for you! Begin now by altering your relationship to time. Begin seeing that it is a sacred gift from God, and how you spend your time is your sacred contract with God. This is what I call being your "God Self on earth." I'm going to teach you a way to manage your commitments, values and priorities - your 'Self' - in relation to time, and that system is called The Sacred System of Energy Management.

Self Management is not time management.

How do you start "managing yourself" in a way that is fulfilling, meaningful, and effective? First, get clear on what you value and desire. Each desire is God expressing His desires in and through you. Unless what you are doing reflects your most deeply held desires and values, you will never experience inner peace. Managing yourself in alignment with your values brings grace and ease to your life.

Step One: Create an 'All of It' List.

How do you begin? One way is to recognize that all that we want to do and experience in life is not infinite. It may feel infinite, because there are so many opportunities in life. Write down everything that you want to be, have or experience in this lifetime, as well as all of the tasks and duties you perform and provide on a daily basis. This list, your "All of It List", will be your unique expression of your God Self on earth and an expression of your vision, values, commitments and priorities. I have had the opportunity to do this exercise with numerous people over the years, and have found the lists are fun and exciting to read. The items range from the everyday (get a haircut, an oil change, commute), to desired lifestyles (spend more time with family, have work be optional, spend winters in a tropical climate, own a sports car), to desired contributions (be a leader in my spiritual community, double the size of my business), to uniquely desired experiences (swim with wild dolphins, hike the Pacific Coast Trail, spend a month in Hawaii).

Step Two: Create your Sacred Contract.

The next step is to go through your "All of It List" and highlight the items that comprise your daily life, such as work, meetings, commuting, daily spiritual practices, and personal care and fitness activities.

Go to your scheduling system (I recommend you use an electronic system), and be sure that each of these items is reflected in your schedule in the specific time that it occurs. For any event that is repeated, use the "recurring event" function so that it shows up automatically in the appropriate time slot.

You are now building your "Sacred Contract." This is an opportunity to train yourself to begin relating to time a contract between you and God.

Ultimately, the goal is that you only put things on your schedule that are a reflection of your Highest Self. You may not be able to operate this way immediately if you are tolerating things that need to change, such as enduring a job or commute that are not in alignment with your Self expression. Relating to your schedule as a Sacred Contract will be the impetus for you to begin eliminating things that are a drain on your life force energy.

After you've entered all recurring events, input all other items which you are currently committed to in your schedule. Most people make the mistake of entering only things such as face to face appointments and meetings. That is better than nothing, but it leaves the majority of your work unaccounted. In this system, you account for all of your commitments. So if your work includes needing to write reports or proposals, you place time in your Sacred Contract (i.e. schedule) to write the report or proposal. If your vocation includes needing to do research on your product or industry, you schedule the time to research. If your marketing needs to be upgraded and you need to look at some web sites of other businesses in your field, schedule time to look at the web sites. This approach to managing commitments frees you from disempowering "should's" and "ought to's" which are an enormous energy drain! People beginning to use this system discover two things: everything takes more time than they estimated, and they have far more commitments than time allows. Both point to the need for greater awareness, alignment with one's values in relation to time.

Step Three: Set Your Sacred Intentions

The third step is to go back to your "All of It List" and highlight the items that you currently dream of doing 'some day' – the visions and desires that you do not currently have the means or a plan to accomplish. This is your "Sacred Intentions List." Sacred Intentions refer to the fact that these are things you intend to do, be, have or experience, but they are not currently goals with a step-by-step action plan. These are intentions set out before God – the first step towards realization. As you move into setting each one as a goal, or turning it into an action plan, it comes off the list.

Step Four: Regularly Review the Sacred System

A word to the wise: the Sacred System is only effective if you implement and live it.

Likely, you will initially be inputting experiences which are not in alignment with your vision of your highest Self. A critical next step is to be clear with yourself and other people involved and "un-commit" from energy draining activities. Keep doing this until your Sacred Contract truly reflects you and becomes a source of life giving energy.

Daily Review: Review your Sacred Contract (schedule) at the end of each day to see if you completed everything you committed to doing. If not, simply move the item forward to when you will commit to accomplishing it. Look to your next day and see if you need to make any alterations. If so, make the necessary adjustments and end your day mentally prepared. Once you practice this, you will see that it takes about 10 minutes to review your day. You no longer need a "to do" list because you place them all in your schedule. If you work in a fast-paced environment, it may be useful to keep a log of needed actions and communications, and then schedule them into your Sacred Contract at the end of each day.

We all have experiences that I call "life coming at you" – times that despite our best efforts, we just don't complete something. Follow this simple rule of thumb: for every item in your Sacred Contract, you can only reschedule it three times. When the fourth time comes up, if you cannot accomplish the item, ask yourself: "Am I really committed to this?" If the answer is "yes", do it. If the answer is "not really", take it off your schedule. If the answer is, "I think I can", simply place the item on your Sacred Intentions list and come back to it if it is truly yours to do.

The goal of the Sacred System is to generate higher level consciousness: high energy people being their 'God self on earth', living in alignment with their vision and values. As we train ourselves to do this, and further our conscious evolution, the more humanity will transform.

Jackie Woodside, LICSW is a clinical social worker in private practice and a business coach for small business owners and entrepreneurs. She has been coaching people around managing their commitments and increasing productivity in alignment with one's higher self for the past 15 years. She creates and conducts courses and workshops that propel people along their spiritual path, being their "God Self on earth." Jackie can be reached at Jwoodside@aol.com or 508-616-9555.

CHAPTER 17

Setbacks Versus Opportunities: Different or the Same?

Helena Wozniak

An old proverb teaches, "All roads lead to Rome," which means that there are many different ways of accomplishing what you set out to do. Once we figure out WHAT we want, most of us believe that there is only one way to achieve it - the way we know. We often decide to only undertake the things we know how to do, thus limiting ourselves to our current ability.

To help you understand, I will tell you the story of one of my business ventures, namely opening a ladies high fashion store. To finance the business, I mortgaged my house - a big risk for a single, hard-working mother of two, newly immigrated to Canada.

During the late 1980's, Canada was still very conservative in comparison to Europe. I put a business plan together, contacted European suppliers, determined when they planned their sample sales, found a store for lease, and I was ready to realize my dream.

The only thing I wasn't sure of was the interior decoration. I wanted it to be unique, warm and inviting. A friend of mine had just remarried and his wife, an artist, offered help in exchange for shares in the store. I was so grateful that I agreed without hesitation.

In time, I signed the lease and jumped on a plane to Europe, leaving her in charge of decor. We discussed budget and I believed that both of us were clear about the amount of the money we had to make our business a success.

When I returned, I was surprised and a little overwhelmed at the luxurious look of our little store. My immediate question of her was "How much did it cost?" When I heard her answer, I wished I hadn't asked. She had spent all the money available on decorating! There was nothing left to pay for the clothes I had ordered from Europe. We had a beautiful store, but nothing to sell.

I tried to arrange some additional loans, but after three months I was forced to sublease the store, sell the house and move my children to a government-subsidized apartment.

Two lessons I learned:

1. Always stay in charge of your plans; never let anyone else realize them for you. Be yourself and avoid imitating anything or anyone.
2. If you need help, ask, but always clarify detailed instructions covering the "what," "when," and "how much?" aspects.

Learn from others, but believe that only you have the power to achieve your desires. If you can "dream it up" you can overcome all obstacles to realizing that dream. There will be setbacks, but only to slow you down to focus your attention on the areas you need to learn more about.

You cannot walk on mountain peaks your whole life. No matter how hard you try, there will be days that result in frustration and failure. You need to walk through the valley to get to the next peak – that's all there is to it!

There is no better education than learning through adversity. Every loss contains its own lesson on how to improve your performance the NEXT time. Face the truth and learn from past mistakes, but do not let them hold you back from making a new mistake.

You must persist in finding your own way to Rome. We all need the experience of adversity, and its wondrous ability to draw our dormant talent to the surface. Never again feel sorry for yourself too long so that you miss a new idea coming to your mind. Even the most beautiful gems are polished with friction. Understand that drudgery's job is to reveal the treasures of your mind; to help you find *other* ways of doing.

Never say you *cannot*. Instead, say you *will not* and ask for help. You always have a choice. When you replace the words *I can't* with *I won't*, you place yourself in charge, replacing fear with confidence.

When you're holding onto the past, particularly when you're focusing on the worst, you are preventing your energy from moving forward. You lack gratitude in your life. Set your energy free and use the past only to ponder on what you want.

When things arise in your business that you do not like or wish to happen again, ask yourself: What is it that you DO want to happen? Let the setback be a trigger, not a focus, of your thinking. You cannot take action on a negative statement. Your focus needs to be on the positive in order to turn a setback into a forward action.

You need to find the guidance within yourself. It is not what you think needs to be done, nor is it what others have told you to do. It is all about how you FEEL about what you do. Every time you make a decision, ask yourself, "How do I feel about this? Good or bad?" If you start to qualify your reason for feeling one way or the other, it is probably not the right decision. You do not have peace of mind, and you need to ask yourself why you do not feel good about your decision. Be honest with yourself and make the decision that feels right.

Trust that there are no setbacks in life, only the divine guidance to do things a different way.

What happens to a river if suddenly its flow is blocked? It becomes stagnant and not appealing as the river is accustomed to its momentum. The river has two options: Become a pond or a lake... or build enough energy to flow over or around the obstruction.

If your business suddenly becomes stagnant, you need to understand that you have a choice. This is your choice, not the circumstance's choice. Take the time to be grateful, as it only slows you down to allow you to make things better.

Instead of pressing a panic button, be grateful for the guidance and ask yourself:

1. Are you enthusiastic about your product or services?
2. Do you use your own products or services?
3. How do they work for you?
4. Are your people enthusiastic about the products or services they deliver?
5. Are you providing products or services that still serve others?

As a Conscious Entrepreneur you must maintain your power of positive motivation in life, in order to direct others in your company who sometimes may struggle. You must inspire and encourage them to be fully awake and aware of their impact on your business and the people your business is serving.

Starts feeling good about what happened to you, remembering that <u>you always have a choice.</u> You should start with:

1. Being grateful that you were stopped,
2. Test your business yourself; do not rely on others; ask yourself how you feel about it,
3. Ask your employees to do the same; listen to their feedback,
4. Ask your customers how they feel about your product or service,
5. Think how you feel about all the feedback you received and your own experience,
6. Do not take immediate action; take time to feel your challenges,
7. Write them down, good and bad.

You assessed your business, identified all that does feel good or not. Now, change every negative statement into a positive. For example: "We often mis-ship our products" should be changed to "We will deliver products accurately."

Now consider this: Can you, your business or your people deliver improvements right now... or ever? Take a second look at your list and ask yourself, "Do I believe that my business provides value to my clients?"

If you answer NO, change your business. Just as a blocked river can become a pond or lake that is home for different species, figure out how you can change what you offer to serve new customers. According to Peter Druker, "The only way you can manage change is to create it."

If the answer is YES, like the blocked river, build your energy to overcome obstacles. Look for new ways to serve your customers or look for the different ways to deliver your goods and services. Build an action plan for every statement that you changed from negative to positive. It should be as detailed as possible. It does not have to be complex, but you <u>must make a decision</u> and it must be followed by action.

Remember the person who perpetually hesitates and cannot decide which one of the two things to do usually does neither! Identify your choices, make your decision and take focused action.

Never do many things indifferently; commit and stay focused; never aim in a general direction. Always be sure about what you want to accomplish. If you shoot an arrow in a general direction, it will not wander around until it finds its target. You need to aim it precisely at the mark.

As a *Conscious Entrepreneur*, it is your responsibility to have the courage to believe that you have the power to turn any adversity into a benefit. Thus, you have the ability to profit from past mistakes. Be grateful for them. Setbacks are your greatest opportunity. Do not be blind to them.

Helena Wozniak is a coach and a writer, leading diverse individuals in a highly competitive market to establish themselves at a better level. She is continually exploring new ways to integrate her spiritual understandings with strategic business tactics. To receive her quarterly newsletter, sign up at her website at www.spiritual-mind.com. She has been a sailor on the high sea of personal development and spirituality for the last twenty years.

PART II:

Living Your Full Potential

CHAPTER 18

Resistance is Futile...
and a Doorway to Freedom!

Gaye Abbott

"Do not follow where the path may lead. Go instead where there is no path and leave a trail. Only those who risk going too far can possibly find out how far one can go."

– T.S. ELIOT

It wasn't long ago that I sold off everything I owned for the second time and drove across country with a girlfriend from Vermont, back towards the West coast where I was born. This decision was another movement in a three-year history of searching for meaning and my hearts desire as I shed identities, rushing head long towards my 60th year of life. Most of the past endeavors, both professionally and personally, no longer held any allure. What was it that was driving me? What larger action was being called for? My life as I knew it, with all of the inner resistance and security based thinking, was about to change dramatically.

It is at pivotal life moments such as these that the most opportunity seems to reside. The question is, will an individual step out and up into what most likely will be unknown and most often terribly uncomfortable territory, or will they resist and stagnate in a place of what is perceived as security? I have learned so eloquently that for a conscious entrepreneur, resistance is not only futile, but can be a catalyst for manifesting goals and attaining success in all of life's moments. In the realm of electricity, resistance is described as "the opposition of a body or substance to current *(life energy)* passing through it, resulting in a change of electrical energy into heat *(catalyst)* or another form of energy." In other words, the potential for greater or a more life giving result! In biology, it can mean the capacity of an organism to defend against disease, or to withstand the effects of a harmful physical or environmental agent. This means the inherent ability of an organism to resist harmful influences.

Thus we have two processes going on at once – the transformation itself, and the organism's biological imperative to survive no matter what. Where is the tipping point that will shift an organism – you or me – towards transformation? This is the process that has the potential to guarantee not just survival, but growth, thriving, and a new found perspective and awareness. Starting one's own business, or pursuing a life long dream or passion, happens to be one of those vehicles for bringing up what feels like tons of resistance, yet also offers unlimited opportunities to uncover the confidence one was born with, but perhaps lost in bits and pieces along the way.

If you are like me, you have perceived resistance either as a bad thing - preventing you from doing what you want - or as a great survival mechanism protecting you from harm. Based on some recent experiences, I now perceive and experience resistance as an energy that has the potential to take one into freedom – to live life fully, consciously, wildly, and on purpose. Reviewing the last 6 months since moving to Oregon, I can honestly say that resistance has been a transformer in every aspect of my life. In fact, I've come to recognize resistance as an Aikido-like collaborator that assists me to shed old beliefs and patterns (ways of thinking and acting) that feel to be solidly standing in the way, and help me to regain/uncover the innate confidence that has always been there. People with high self-confidence typically have little fear of the unknown, are able to stand up for what they believe in, and have the courage to risk embarrassment, i.e. mistakes.

Enter now two worlds that are distinctly different, yet hold some common universal principles that exemplify personal resistance (*mine!*) and where it can take you. One had resistance hiding within it, and the other, in the form of extreme judgment, prevented any action ever being taken. Although both are physically based, don't be fooled – they hold all of the elements necessary to break through into living life on purpose, with passion and joy, while thriving (grow luxuriantly!).

These two vehicles for "resistance training" entered my life through different doorways. Both continue to be support systems for confidence and the unraveling of contracted security based and protective thinking based in the illusion of fear.

First came something that I am passionate about. For as long as I can remember, I have loved movement in my body – especially dance. Having taken some ballroom dance lessons and also having explored contact improv, African and contra dancing, my favorite expression was just free form – let go and move! When I am dancing I feel free - as if everything in me is open and alive. Several months ago I was sitting at an outdoor festival drawn to the type of music that makes me come alive to all my senses. What unfolded was a demonstration of Cuban Casino salsa music in a form call Rueda (circle partner dance). I could hardly stay in my seat, wanting to join in with the complex moves these couples were passionately showing us. What struck me and pulled me in (besides the music), was the aliveness, vibrant energy, passion, sensuality and open smiling faces. My body, heart and soul said a resounding YES! to these classes that were offered at a local studio, and within a week I was in Level One Cuban Casino salsa class.

Fast forward a couple of months and see me walking into a "hot yoga" or Birkram's yoga class. My judgments and beliefs – yes, you can say extreme resistance here – about this style/form of yoga were so immense that it was amazing that I even went to that first class. Having practiced and studied yoga for over 20 years, and being a yoga teacher/therapist myself, I thought that I *knew* what a yoga practice "should be." Bikram's yoga certainly didn't fit that. Enter a beloved friend who at 69 years old had been practicing this style on and off for a couple of years, and looks and acts many years younger than his stated age. Within the comfort of our friendship, I was able to look at the almost overwhelming resistance to this style and realize that with that much resistant energy, there must be opportunities within for growth. I consciously walked into my first 95 degree room with my friend just a few months ago.

Hopefully I have you curious about the outcome of my saying YES to these new experiences! Hidden resistance gives one the opportunity to take action initially, like I did when signing up for salsa lessons. Within the journey of learning rests unlimited opportunities to hit up against resistance – in this case surrendering to the male lead, and my perfectionism. As each class unfolded through a new level of steps, body placement, and new partners, we each were able to realize that we would learn through the path of mistakes and repetition. Once I learned to laugh at my faux pas's and keep moving forward into more complex moves – and more *fun* – I found a freedom of enjoyment as well as a comfort in my being that kept expanding. I realized that feeling the resistance in my body (oh, how long it took me to relax my arms!) meant that the opportunity for freedom was there as well. Relationship with self, with a partner, and with the group as a whole kept me focused, curious, and determined to mine the depths of letting go, and to follow the wise words of one of the dance instructors – "fake it till you make it."

The "hot yoga" path continues to inform me to do the best I can in the moment, and the confidence, ability, strength, flexibility, deep letting go, and expanded awareness flow from there. Every time I walk into the practice room and feel the heat, I know that for 90 minutes I will be completely and absolutely committed to doing the best I can, and to staying focused with clear concentration and absolute willingness to be present no matter what happens. My commitment of three months of unlimited classes has opened doorways to physical, mental, emotional and spiritual expansion that are there for me because I was willing to say YES to something that I had put up a brick wall against. I am now aware that this was the exact practice that I needed to support me in building and growing my business. The feeling of freedom is immense!

It is through other people that resistance can be worked with *in relationship* instead of reaction. My deepest gratitude to:

- David Neagle, Life Is Now, and my Platinum MasterMind Group (www. davidneagle.com)
- Fred Edward, Elder Extraordinaire
- Christine Kloser, Love Your Life Publishing (www.loveyourlife.com)
- Rumbanana Salsa Troupe (www.rumbanana.org)
- Bikram's Yoga College of India - Corvallis, Oregon (www.BikramYoga-Corvallis.com)

**A Request: The two examples given in this chapter come out of my personal journey. Your individual journey will present other kinds of opportunities that will be perfect for you. Trying to replicate mine could take you away from the very opportunities to grow, transform and live on purpose. Please honor your own unique path and let me know what happens!

Gaye Abbott lives in the Pacific Northwest and offers "resistance training", resources, and muse support for women 50 years of age and beyond. She is moving into her 6th decade wildly free, and committed to women's personal and global confident authentic expression. Sign up for the bi-monthly e-zine, WildlyFreeWomenThrive and receive a FREE report – 9 Secrets to the Art of Embodied Confidence, and 20% off for any products or services. www.WildlyFreeWoman.com (Code: CE77 – one use)

CHAPTER 19

The Triple Win:
I Win... You Win... The World Wins

Tom Feldman, M.A., and Bev Feldman, M.A.

The age of the conscious entrepreneur is upon us precisely because of the trouble we have brought upon ourselves. We hear about these issues daily: global warming, over-fishing, habitat destruction, overpopulation, pollution, exhausting our non-renewable resources, etc. Many of us see and feel these changes now.

We've been studying the role of the conscious entrepreneur in our work with individuals, businesses, and nonprofits. Conscious entrepreneurs have a very bright future doing business by solving problems. They make a profit while in service to humanity and the planet, and serve as examples and leaders to a sustainable future.

Think of it like this: a train leaves the station. The engine that drives the train is today's economic thinking, which puts profits first. But some passengers on the train are realizing that the train's next stop could easily be environmental and social collapse. What to do? The track is already laid: our present rate of consumption of the world's resources is unsustainable.

If we want the train to arrive at a destination with a future, we must take responsibility and unprecedented action: entrepreneurs must get in front of the train and lay down new track.

Who will take the lead to sustainability? Governments will have a role, but we think that business, including the solo practitioner, will be the likely leaders of this new way of thinking. Financial success will be tied with both environmental and social success, and implemented both voluntarily and by law. This is already happening in the European Union.

When business (whether at the level of the corporation, non-profit, or the conscious entrepreneur) makes a profit, insures that its clients win, and that the world is a better place for it, they've put down new track and we call that "The Triple Win."

Business has long used the win/win scenario as an example of a best practice in the sense of being good for both sides. But win/win leaves a lot of latitude: clear cutting a forest may be good for the lumber company and good for its customers and shareholders, but bad for the ecosystem... a win/win/lose. We think that win/win used to be a serviceable idea, but it's not a **big enough** idea: the stakes are higher now than they've ever been. It's the future of humanity, all large mammals and the systems that support us. We can't lose this one.

Triple Win not only includes all the players from win/win, but it puts another seat at the table and another chair in the boardroom for life and the world. Up until now, the world has been ON the table and not AT the table.

Who speaks for the polar bears? Who speaks for the oceans? Who speaks for the Amazon? Who speaks for the poor and the sick? With Triple Win – I Win, You Win, the World Wins -- all of life is included when we as individuals, householders, businesspeople, conscious entrepreneurs and corporations, start to act consistently with the health of the earth in mind. It can be done in many ways, on many fronts

To create a Triple Win, you don't necessarily need to look very far. Just look at the places that the world touches you. Somewhere you are being called to make a difference. And right there, in what calls you, you might lay down new track. Humanity's new destination is one where individuals and societies thrive, systems work, the environment heals, and our shared future is secure.

Let's meet some conscious entrepreneurs who were touched by the world and are out in front of the train.

The Two Million Dollar Bag Man

Andy Keller is a 34-year old regular guy living in Chico, California. A few years ago on an unspectacular day, he got up and drove some yard waste to the County Dump. He couldn't help but see that there were literally hundreds of plastic bags blowing around the landfill. Frankly, every single person who ever came to the dump saw the very same scene, but Andy's the <u>one guy</u> who was moved to do something about it. The future touched him that day.

He'd just been fired from his job as a sales rep for a software company, so he had some time to create a solution. He got an old sewing machine and figured out how to use it. Then he designed a reusable fabric bag that stuffs into its own attached tiny sack. He didn't know if there would be a market for his ChicoBag, but apparently people needed a solution like this… because he's sold hundreds of thousands of them and the company brought in two million dollars in 2007.

Andy's making a profit, he has happy, dedicated customers and employees, but best of all, he's making a living keeping plastic out of the streets, landfills and oceans and showing us a better way as he lays down new track. Triple Win!

(www.ChicoBag.com)

The Big Weed

The future called a young John Roulac the day a truck dumped a load of nuclear waste just nine miles from the family house. That was it: John knew he would spend his life solving environmental problems.

At 22, he wrote a simple book on composting. Today <u>Backyard Composting</u> has sold over a million copies and resulted in municipalities across the country adopting and teaching composting to citizens. John didn't stop there. He discovered industrial hemp, a Swiss-Army knife of a plant unfortunately confused with the psychoactive Cannabis Sativa. This big weed is banned as a commercial crop in the US (but legal in all the other developed countries of the world) despite it's hundreds of uses as food, fuel, renewable paper products (saving forests), and compostable plastics.

So John became an expert and advocate for hemp and took on the US government. He also started a food products company, Nutiva, which makes hemp-based nutrition bars, shakes, and oils using organically-cultivated hemp seed and hemp seed oil that presently has to be grown in Canada though John's working to change that. Nutiva did nearly $7 million in business in 2007. Triple Win.

(www.Nutiva.com)

Weapons of Mass Creation

The Jules Dervaes family demonstrates you can lay down new track right in your own backyard.

These "urban homesteaders" from Pasadena, California, grow over 300 varieties of edible plants that yield in excess of 6,000 pounds of produce a year on a normal-sized city lot! They sell edible flowers, exotic greens, and duck eggs to local restaurants and caterers and their products are in high demand.

Jules and his adult children have supported themselves for 10 years with home micro-agriculture. They produce their own power and brew their own biodiesel in an old water heater using discarded fast food oil. They even have a bicycle-powered blender!

By making a profit, sharing and teaching what they do through self-sufficiency workshops, tours, ecological film screenings, and a content-rich highly trafficked website, the Dervaes' have created an everyman's Triple Win.

(www.PathToFreedom.com)

The Prison MBA

The US Department of Justice in 2006 reported that 1 in every 31 adults was in prison, jail, on probation or out on parole. Catherine Rohr took a tour of a prison and recognized that many inmates were incarcerated precisely because of their entrepreneurial skills, which were criminally-focused. "Take a drug ring,'" she said. "They know all about pricing, timely delivery and customer service. What if we channeled all of that in a positive manner?"

So Catherine founded the Prison Entrepreneurship Program (PEP), a shining example of a social Triple Win.

It's entrance exams, writing assignments, homework and computer training and 350 hours of class time. Volunteer executives work with the men, and students from MBA programs including Harvard and Stanford provide feedback for their business plans. By the end of the class, the men present their full business plans to an executive panel just as they would if pitching their idea to potential investors.

Catherine also created a supportive network of post-release services, everything from picking them up when they are released to helping with social services, housing, jobs, continuing entrepreneurial education and providing access to angel investors. Over 40 businesses have been started. "For most of them, this is the biggest accomplishment of their lives," says Catherine. "It's definitely a business experience but also a personal transformation." With a recidivism rate less than 5% vs. more than 50% nationally, it's a Triple Win.

(www.Pep.org)

The Triple Win and You

Andy Keller makes a living reducing plastic waste. John Roulac makes a living growing a banned weed to provide food, and soon to make paper products that save trees, provide fuel and recyclable plastics. The Dervaes' are making a living supporting family and community by growing healthy and nutritious food and energy with less waste. Catherine Rohr looks inside the pathology of criminals, finds the seed of a healthy entrepreneur and waters it. Each of these people wants a better life for themselves, their clients and the world. They see more broadly. Each is creating a Triple Win in their own way.

Is possibility calling you? Where the world touches you, we hope you will look more broadly than you might have, and find **your** way to lay new track for the Triple Win.

Tom and Bev Feldman have Master's degrees in Global Studies with an emphasis on Sustainability. They coach entrepreneurs and companies to create The Triple Win using The Integral Framework, Spiral Dynamics, and other cutting-edge transformational tools. Tom is CEO of ClearFire Media, Board Chair of The Forge Institute, and teaches at Woodbury University in Burbank, California. Bev Feldman owns her own entrepreneurial business, StarPrompt.TV. For more information on The Triple Win, go to www.TripleWinVision.com.

CHAPTER 20

Stuck in "Job-Job?"
5 Easy Steps to Finding and Following Your True Path

Heather Gray

Does this sound like you? "One day I will pursue my real passions, but right now I need to make money" or "I can't leave my job, it's what pays the bills."

There is nothing worse than feeling trapped by a job-job. (A "Job-Job" is anything you do only for the money. In other words, if you were to win the lottery tomorrow, it would be one of the first things you would stop doing.) Seven years ago, at the age of 32 I left a "job-job" and I have never looked back. The longer I have been outside the confines of the 9 to 5 world, the more ease I have discovered in maintaining a free lifestyle. In fact, one of the most frequent questions I am asked by friends, clients and colleagues is: "When do you work?" I used to feign working harder to fit in, but these days I pass on what I've learned to others, because I truly believe that your purpose is not meant to be squandered at a job that has your heartstrings pulling you in a different direction.

This chapter explores 5 EASY steps that will help you find your way out of the "job-job" and back towards your true path. My hope is that they bring you the miracles that I discovered when I consciously put these steps into practice in my own life.

1. Stop being so busy and create S P A A A A C E

"Your Soul talks to you everyday, but if you are too busy, you cannot hear what it is trying to say."

~ DENISE LINN, AUTHOR OF SOUL COACHING

I don't need to tell you that we live in a fast paced world that prizes productivity and DOING. The mind set we are hypnotized by is "more, more, more" and "you have to work hard to be successful." It is also a paradigm that wreaks havoc on our health if we are constantly pushing and pushing without any 'R&R.' (For some, illness becomes the only way that they allow time for themselves -- not a powerful way to live!)

Let's flip this tired theory on its head and have more by doing LESS. Take a look at your schedule right now. Is there time in there for doing nothing? That's right, nothing! If you are scheduled with back-to-back-to-back appointments, then there will be no room for flow, or the mystery and whispering of your soul to come in. You need to create some space in your daily activities to allow for the feminine flow and to get in the rhythm of your life. Fight the urge to fill up every hour in your schedule with 'doing.'

And I don't mean that you are going to schedule an activity to be your nothing. When I first introduce this concept to some of my clients, they want to count their yoga class or their meditation time as nothing. No, that is not 'nothing.' These are upgraded, spiritually evolved "to do" activities. Yes, they will nurture you, but they are still appointments. The only appointment you want when you are creating SPACE is an appointment with yourself. No plan. You will only know when you arrive there what it is your heart wants you to do (see steps 2-5 for more guidance).

When you get good at this, you can block out entire days for doing NOTHING except to do what feels right. Sort of a mini-retreat for you, where you don't know where the destination is, but only what your heart is telling you to do next. This is when your soul will come in and grab you by the hand and take you leaps and bounds beyond anything your mental "doing" self would have ever conceived for you.

2. Look for and notice coincidences, synchronicities, and repetitive thoughts

When you create space and are not running from one thing to the next, that is when you will notice the signs and synchronicities around you. The Universe will nudge you or confirm that yes, you are heading in the right direction, or "Hey, notice this--it's important."

I have a friend who when she drives makes a point of noticing license plates, road signs and slogans on the sides of trucks. For her, these are messages from the Universe. When she was working on her music album, a license plate saying "Rock Star" was a great thumbs up message for her to keep going!

What signs do you see around yourself? Are there any synchronicities or coincidences that have been happening to you? Keep a journal for recording these occurrences and your insights about them. Also, take notice of any repetitive thoughts that are coming to you. Often we receive guidance through these quiet, but consistent ideas. The more you take notice, the more your soul will communicate through your surroundings and your own thoughts.

3. Stop "should-ing" yourself

Should's are guilt dressed up as Puritan work ethic... and they creep up on you. One day I was squeezing in a quick run to the grocery store that took me along the street where my gym was located and I caught myself thinking "You should go to the gym." But the thought was even nastier than that, it was more like, "You should go to the gym, you lazy bum." Ahh! As if it wasn't enough that I was already rushing to get one thing done, this "SHOULD" slammed down on me about what I was not doing. That 'should' voice had no appreciation for what I was getting accomplished and offered a never ending barrage of what still 'should' be getting done.

When you catch yourself Should-ing, say to yourself, "Thank you for sharing and I COULD do that, but right now I choose not to." It works magic and puts the power back in your control. It also helps you get in touch with what you really want to be doing (important to our next step), and not the slave to some Puritan sitting on your shoulder that beats you up. When we keep following all the should's in our life, we don't even know what we want to do!

4. Follow your heart. What do YOU want to do next?

Now that you have created some space, are watching for signs and have stopped hounding yourself about what you should be doing, notice what the intuitive part of yourself is expressing. Ask yourself (and be honest), what do you really want to do now? Maybe you want to simply take your favorite book and go to a local coffee shop and read. Do that. Or maybe you are craving some time in nature. Get outside.

You only need to take hold of the next rung on the ladder. You do not need to see the top. Our guidance is often just what to do next. You can never see the whole journey from your current vantage point. All is not revealed at once - just do what is next for you to do. The more you do what's next and what feels right, the more your path opens up and takes you to the most amazing places. So get started on your own magical journey, which is truly unique and perfect for you.

5. Raise your vibration through inspiration

Get to know what inspires you. What are the things that consistently put you in a happier, good vibes place? When you are sad, depressed, upset, tired or lethargic, it is difficult to be in touch with the magic flow of the universe. You need to raise your vibration so that you are in sync with that higher part of yourself that is waiting to open doors and show you the way. If you are complaining about someone, beating yourself up about something or just in a funky funk, then you cannot access the guidance that is available. In fact, you should AVOID making decisions and taking important actions from a negative place. Do what ever it takes to get you feeling better.

Here are some of my favorites (borrow and add your own): journaling; writing up a gratitude list; walking in nature; listening to my favorite tunes; reading a book by an inspirational author (I always carry an inspiring book with me); taking a personal growth workshop; wearing something that makes me feel great; praying; watching Oprah; sending silent blessings to people, or seeing an uplifting movie.

Begin adding inspirational practices into your life today. Notice what makes you feel better and surround yourself with these things. This will help you along the way, especially when you are entering into the sacred space you create from less doing.

FINALLY GET STARTED TODAY!

Magic happens when you have that extra time and you wander through a bookstore and find that perfect book. It's when you walk on a new street because you felt like it, and end up running into someone you haven't seen in years who just happens to be the perfect connection to something you are working on or your next hot date!

Here's to loads of magic and joy unfolding in the spaces of your life!

Heather Gray is a certified Soul Coach, Reiki Master, Holistic Health Counselor and Author of Real Girl, Real World: A Guide to Finding Your True Self (Seal Press 2005). Her deepest desire is to help others find and follow their true path while creating joy and abundance along the way. Go to: www.spreadyourwingsandinspire.com for a FREE subscription to "Spread Your Wings…and Inspire," revealing EASY, clear ways to thrive and prosper by following your true path.

CHAPTER 21

From Passion to Profit

Deborah Gudelsky

I know that I have one of the best jobs in the world. If you had told me 10 years ago what I would be doing, I would have struggled to believe it. Many of my life's experiences, the caring and commitment of wonderful people, and some consistent risk taking, all unfolded over time. This was all exquisitely woven together to create the beautiful fabric of my life today.

If you don't believe your creative passion can become a business, please read my story. If you are feeling frustrated, defeated, or unclear about how your creative passion can become a business, let me share the colorful road that led to my dream. You might be thinking the idea just popped into my mind like a beautifully wrapped gift from the universe, all complete and neatly packaged. It wasn't quite delivered that way.

My company, *Interior Intentions*, manifested from many life experiences – some at times difficult, challenging, and painful. What I have learned is that when you are moving through any of these life chapters, if you maintain the practice of specific principles, you will gain forward progress, wisdom, and joy. I believe that life-changing personal, business, and spiritual growth can be gleaned from hardships, mistakes, and life's adversity with the continued use of three practices. These golden rules are: the sustained, positive vision of a dream with goals to get there; a continuing support system; and the persistence of risk-taking.

Rule One

It is important to know or discover what your dreams are, and this is where my story began. I was just divorced and embarking on recovery from the pain and trauma of a major life change. "What do you dream of doing with your life?" asked my psychologist. I was really unnerved by this question, partly because I don't remember anyone ever asking me this, and partly because I didn't know the answer.

With some introspection and the guidance of the psychologist, old dreams began to surface. Did you ever lie in bed at night when you were a child, trying to fall asleep, and begin to imagine what your life would be like when you were older? I remembered having the feeling of absolutely knowing at the age of only 7 that I was here to be an artist. This was my divine path. Wonderful! But how would I get from this moment of discovery and joy to being a financially successful professional artist?

One of my challenges was the overwhelming chatter of the "monkeys" in my head. You know – those negative thoughts that wish you could stop. "You're too old", "You don't know how to do this", "Artist's don't make any money", and "You're not good enough or smart enough." Lots of big loud monkeys.

I stepped away from those voices to think about what it might feel like if I didn't pursue my visions. How would it feel to be a person who hadn't tried to realize their dreams? The feelings of sadness and regret that surfaced became bigger than the fear of taking the risk to begin something new.

Here are some things I've learned about the monkeys. These voices come in and clutter my mind, but they are never in my heart. They may have a voice, but they don't get the final decision about my dreams – only my heart and soul have that privilege. If you let these doubting, negative energies make your choices, you cannot see your dreams or the road to get there. It's important to be able to continually *visualize* your dream and *feel* the benefits of reaching them, because the energy that comes from this ensures moving forward.

Once I had my dream, I made a map of how to get there. If there is a plan to accompany your vision, then there are many forward movements you can begin to accomplish. One at a time, always envisioning your dream, take these important steps. The more you do this, the more likely you are to quiet the monkey chatter, and the closer your dream is to becoming reality. I got going with my plan. I put together a portfolio, applied to art school, was accepted, and began to work towards a fine art degree.

Rule Two

Art school was rewarding and fun, but critiques of my work usually left my ego notably bruised, and would inevitably dim my dreams. This is when I employed my second practice, the participation in a supportive group. It began with enrolling in a personal growth workshop that was conducted over a long weekend. About a year after that, I did another one just for women.

I learned and practiced new tools to help with future difficulties and set-backs. I realized that I was not alone with my dreams or my negative voices. One of the most valuable gifts from this was becoming part of a *circle* of women. We gathered together for continued support for many months after the workshop. When you declare your dreams and goals to a supportive group, you are then being affirmed and held by the collective. The result of sharing your vision is that you are not alone in your journey and you have help to reach your goals.

This support always gives me the energy and confidence for the responsibility of getting goals accomplished. The comfort of feeling connected, of being lifted and lifting others, loved and loving others, the sharing of our dreams, moving towards them, and then reaching the milestones in the testimony of others is what nourishes me and keeps me continuing to go to the circle.

Being part of a circle also becomes ritual. As a protected place to share and work through the range of feelings we have as humans, this is another important value of meeting in a circle and having sustained rituals. We don't have to be alone with the weight of all that we feel, and we are offered solutions if we want them. I have been in many circles over the past 15 years, and not always just with women. If you can't find one, you can always start your own.

Rule Three

An unexpected phone call then took my life in a different direction. My father was diagnosed with cancer shortly after retiring and moving away from the area. Treatments and medicines did not work and my father asked if he could come live with me. His request both flattered and terrified me because I had no experience with end of life matters. This is when I began to see the value in taking risks.

After my fathers passing, I wondered about my own life. What did I want my life to mean or stand for? I wanted a way to make a difference with my art and honor my father, so I transferred to another college so I could begin adding art therapy courses to my degree.

During a semester break from school, I took a beading workshop at a holistic learning center. A new passion began as I realized I could use my artistic skills to create beautiful small pieces of art in a short time. Not long after that, I heard of a small organization that was promoting the arts in healthcare settings. I attended one of their meetings at a local hospital. I came home wondering how I could use my beading in the hospital, and offer art with personal meaning that would improve their experience or their life. Yes, the "monkeys" jumped right in on this one. "You don't *have* any experience"; "You don't *have* your art therapy degree", and "Why would they hire *you*?" I put their negative chatter aside and set up an interview the next day. I began working at the hospital the following week with my idea that I named "*Spiritbeads.*"

The experience of caring for my father, changing schools, trying new art forms, and asking for a job were all risks for me. If I hadn't taken these risks, I would not have gained the opportunity to see the breadth of what I could learn, create and accomplish.

As it turns out, the sum of all my risk taking experiences proved to help me with this rewarding job. This was an important insight for me. If I look at all my life experiences individually, they may not seem so significant, but when I string them all together, it has a bigger and more rewarding outcome.

I've been working in hospitals for 4 years with "*Spiritbeads.*" My dream continues to expand with the launching of my own artwork that I named "*Spiritseeds*", beaded botanicals whose images, symbolism and titles remind people to live with their intentions first. I started a company called *Interior Intentions* that includes both arts.

Each day I envision my dreams and continue to list the steps to my goals as they expand and increase my income. I consistently go to the different circles I'm in for the support and networking it provides. I keep taking risks. Wouldn't you like to be living with your intentions first?

Deborah Gudelsky is the founder of Interior Intentions, a unique company honoring the inner intentions we desire for ourselves or for others through two different lines of art. Spiritbeads is a service providing expressive art workshops, and Spiritseeds is a product line of beaded botanical art to purchase. Discover more at www.InteriorIntentions.net, and download our complimentary color symbolism book. Contact Deborah by email at InteriorIntentions@verizon.net or 301-320-5155.

CHAPTER 22

How to Use Your Divine Footprint™ to Leverage the Law of Attraction and Make More Money in Your Business

Cheryl Harris

You are unique. Your personality has an energy that is different from everyone else on the planet. It's important that your business reflects your personality and uses your unique energy as its foundation.

Everything in the universe is energy. This is absolutely not an accident; it's actually a very clever stroke of brilliance. The universe reads your energy, finds a match and responds in kind. This means you are in fact rewarded for expressing your uniqueness in the world. We call this system the Law of Attraction.

When you're using the Law of Attraction in your favor, you're in the flow. It's like a strong river current gathering everything you want and delivering it to you. You enjoy your ride down river just as much as you enjoy reaching your destination. When you're not aligned with the Law of Attraction, you will either intuitively sense or physically see indicators that your business is not reaching its full potential. Furthermore, this disconnect causes your joy and happiness to diminish. It's like a dam in the river disrupting the natural flow of the current.

To maximize the benefits of the Law of Attraction, you must first acknowledge what I call your Divine Footprint™. The foundation of your Divine Footprint™ is the spiritual presence, the spark from the Divine that resides in each of us. It also includes attributes that are unique to you; your innate talents that show up instinctively, spark your curiosity and ignite your passion. It includes your likes, dislikes, and your unique definitions for success and joy. The world is your oyster when you acknowledge the Divine presence that resides within you, and marry that presence with the uniqueness of your talents, your passion, your likes and dislikes, etc. while remaining open to all possibilities.

The innate talents of my Divine Footprint™ are about energy and strategies. I'm curious about every aspect of universal energy and I study it from every angle. On the other hand, the strategist in me never sleeps. My mind is constantly making order out of chaos, seeing the big picture, finding alternative routes, and connecting the dots. Being a strategist is so natural for me that I sometimes forget that everyone else isn't wired the same way I am.

Where does your brilliance shine? What are the unique attributes of your Divine Footprint™?

Creating an Energetically Congruent Business (ECB)

An ECB uses a strategy that resonates with who you are as a person, what makes you unique, and what you stand for as a company. It allows you to use your business to further your self-expression in the world. The more you allow your business to express who you are, the more unique your business becomes. No matter how much anyone tries, they will never be able to duplicate your business, or you. When properly created and implemented, an ECB uses your Divine Footprint™ to keep you in the flow and achieve the results you desire. You will also attract the right clients, make more money and enjoy every aspect of your life in the process. Success will find you. You will never again have to go searching for it.

Go with the Flow

Just like water in a river quickly redirects itself around a boulder, when you are in the flow you too will quickly move beyond situations that would have previously created obstacles in your path. When you are in the flow it means you are walking in step with your Divine Footprint™. This causes the energy you transmit out into the universe to resonate on a very high frequency. You're always connected to the Divine Energy. But resonating at a high frequency allows you to effortlessly receive the intuitive guidance that provides personal answers to your questions and solutions to your problems. It will inspire you with monumental ideas for how you can joyfully express your uniqueness in the world, while illuminating a path every step of the way that will allow you to achieve more than you could achieve on your own. Potential obstacles may still appear, but when you are in the flow you will glide right past them, taking notice of their boldness while not allowing them to slow you down.

Here are some ECB strategies that will keep you in the flow:
- Make a commitment to yourself and your business. Hold the vision of your commitment in your consciousness.
- Build your business on the platform of your Divine Footprint™ and allow your unique gift and your natural brilliance to shine.
- Focus your attention on any and all evidence that the abundance and success you desire is occurring
- Trust the Divine guidance of your intuition and take action on what you feel is the next logical step.

Don't Swim Up Stream

When it feels like you're swimming upstream, this is a definite sign that you are not walking in step with your Divine Footprint™. You're no longer in the flow. You're fighting the current and working much harder than you need to. This type of energy creates a dam in your natural flow and inhibits your ability to attract what you desire.

Here are some indicators that you may be swimming up-stream. I've also provided suggestions on how to get back in the flow:

- You're internal dialogue starts creating doubt, worry, and fear that diminish who you are and what is possible for you.
  - Hold the faith! You would not have been given an idea if you do not

also have what it takes to achieve it. Surround yourself with people and environments that support you and your vision.

- You're doing everything "they" say you have to do to successfully market your business, but you still aren't getting new clients.
  - Align your marketing activities with your gifts, personality, and the things you enjoy doing. Listen to your intuitive voice and take actions that feel right for you.
- You are reluctant to be yourself when you are with your target market or you are exhausted after spending time with them.
  - Redefine your target market. Your business will be more successful if you spend your time with people that energize you and encourage the full expression of who you are.

Embrace the Waves of the Ripple Effect

When you drop a rock at a rivers edge it creates waves that ripple across the river. Likewise, the energy of your business, relationships, health, and every aspect of your life all ripple across and intermingle with each other. Therefore, you must be energetically congruent in every aspect of your life to reach your highest potential.

Your collective thoughts and beliefs determine the vibration you transmit out into the universe. The frequency of your vibration determines the reality of your life. I call this Astral Advertising™. The good news is that since **you** get to decide what **you** think, feel and believe, **you** are solely responsible for your astral advertisement. This means you can achieve anything you desire. Your astral advertisement controls the level of success in your business, and ultimately the happiness in your life. It's actually quite liberating when you think about it!

When you shut down any aspect of your life, pretend to be someone that you are not, blame others, or do anything that feels like you are swimming upstream, you are sending out incongruent energetic astral advertisements. The universe reads your energy, finds a match, and responds in kind. That means anytime you are energetically incongruent, you will transmit and receive something different than what you want.

Take Advantage of the Eddy

Most rivers have rapids. They include obstacles such as huge boulders, dangerous undertows, and extremely fast water. Like a swimmer bobbing through river rapids, there may be times when you find yourself rushing through your business. You're focused solely on keeping your head above water, your mouth closed and avoiding the boulders. You're so intent on surviving that you're no longer listening to your intuitive voice or consciously engaging the Laws of Attraction. It's critical to find your eddy where you can step back and take a breath. This means taking time away from your business and going on vacation for fun, relaxation and rejuvenation. Without this rest, your energy will wane and you will send an astral advertisement that requires the universe to deliver more of the same. The time away is time well spent because it keeps you in energetic integrity.

The absolute best way to maximize your success is to keep yourself energetically congruent with your Divine Footprint™. Living authentically keeps your energy resonating on a level that transmits the most powerful astral advertisement for receiving the happiness and success you desire. Do this by building your business and living your life around your Divine Footprint™, listening to and trusting your intuition and taking action on what you intuitively know is the next logical step.

Cheryl Harris is an international keynote speaker, certified coach and business strategist. She teaches entrepreneurs and executives how to shift their energy to leverage the full power of the Law of Attraction and get the results they want in their business, relationships, and life… in 90 days or less. To learn more about her programs and receive her free Special Report, The Truth about the Law of Attraction: How to FINALLY Get the Results You Want!, please visit www.ConsciousCreationsInc.com.

CHAPTER 23

Use Soul Power to Overcome Obstacles and Create the Life of Your Dreams

Bonnie Hutchinson

BE YOUR BIG SELF. YOU ARE BEAUTIFUL.

So there I was, wondering whether and how I could make the switch from the consulting business that had supported me for many years, to a new business more aligned with my current passions.

And there I was, driving through heavy traffic.

And there it was – the billboard. All black background. Huge white letters.

As I noticed the billboard, the first thing I thought was, "There is no logo and no call to action. What kind of a billboard is that?"

And a nanosecond later, just as I passed the sign, the words registered. BE YOUR BIG SELF. YOU ARE BEAUTIFUL.

I am not making this up. Those were the words on the billboard.

Sometimes the Universe is not subtle.

I'll come back to the billboard, but first, some context.

Like many conscious entrepreneurs, I have been on a spiritual journey for a while now. Whatever else I have been doing in my business and personal life, the passion that drives me is spiritual growth.

I am a spiritual junkie. I have devoured books, gone to workshops, met psychics and channels, worked with master teachers and healers, and had messages from past life experiences. One of my most important teachers taught me to discern what kind of energy was in situations in my life, and how to change and uplift the energy.

I also learned that, like people, organizations and businesses have a soul and energy of their own. In my organizational consulting business, I often saw organizations playing out the same dramas that individuals did.

I began quietly to weave spiritual practices into my work as an organizational consultant. And as I continued to incorporate this spiritual work, I stood back in awe and watched miracles happen.

Long-term conflicts were resolved. Organizations shifted from "scarcity mentality" to abundance. Obstacles that had stopped good things from happening simply dissolved. Funds appeared. Dreams became reality. My client organizations were able to provide far more benefit to the world than they had before, and they were having more fun too.

I didn't talk about the secret spiritual work I did. I knew that my focus on the energy and spirit of situations helped to create miraculous outcomes, but I was also aware that for many of my clients, my "woo woo" beliefs and practices would seem strange or even unacceptable.

So I quietly did my spiritual work behind the scenes. I was content with my own inner knowledge of how I accomplished what I did. I loved my work and my clients.

Yet gradually I realized I was having less fun. I was less motivated and energized. If I were brutally honest, I would even acknowledge being tired and cranky sometimes. That was not what I expected of myself as a conscious entrepreneur committed to serving the highest good of my clients.

I no longer wanted to work on projects to achieve other people's objectives. I no longer wanted my spiritual work to be a silent gift. I wanted my work to <u>be</u> the spiritual practices that created magic for my clients. That was what my soul yearned for. That would be my highest creative expression now.

Like many other conscious entrepreneurs, I knew where I wanted to go, but how could I make the transition?

The answer was blindingly obvious. In fact, I was blind to it for a long time! Gradually it came to me, a millimeter at a time. I could use the very techniques I had developed to create magic for others, to develop my own new business called Soul Power. However, first I had to think through all that I had learned and practiced for over twenty years of running a business and being on a spiritual journey. I realized that I always used the same seven steps to create miracles for my organizational clients – and for my own life.

Seven steps for tapping into Soul Power

1. **Set your intention** – The clearer your statement of intention the better. Write it down. Say it out loud. Let it sink into your mind, body and emotions. Then make it even stronger. Consciously choose to make this intention a reality in your life.

2. **Align with your soul's highest wisdom** – Your soul wants only your happiness, and your soul knows your life purpose. Sit quietly for a few minutes and consciously open yourself to be guided by your soul's deepest and highest wisdom.

3. **Magnetize your intention** – In my spiritual travels, I learned many techniques that help to attract whatever is needed or desired in a particular situation. Imagine yourself as a magnet, effortlessly drawing in what is perfect for right now.

4. **Dissolve blocks and fears** – When you decide to take a new step, it is not unusual for all your limiting beliefs and fears to rise up in a deafening chorus of resistance. I am eternally grateful to the teacher who taught me techniques to work directly with the energy of fear – regardless of what the fear is about. If you clear out the energy of fear, then whatever the fear is about tends to disappear as well. That in turn helps to dissolve any other obstacles.

5. **Raise your vibration** – Every thought, emotion and physical environment has a certain vibration or frequency. Your dreams and desires have a frequency. The purpose of raising your vibration is to consciously shift emotions, thoughts and physical environments so their frequency synchronizes with what you intend to create.

6. **Build momentum** – Like a ball rolling down a hill, once a dream begins

to manifest, it starts to pick up speed and force. A little nudge now and then can help it along.

7. **Celebrate and appreciate** – Success breeds success. Appreciation and gratitude are magnetic. When you notice and celebrate small and big successes, that helps attract even more things to celebrate and appreciate.

These seven steps are macro and micro. They can apply to a big dream and they can apply to a tiny task. When I look back at all the times I have manifested perfection – for my clients or myself – these are the steps I have followed, the soul actions I have taken.

I had already proven this system with dozens of organizational clients over the years. I knew it was the source of countless miraculous achievements.

I laughed out loud on the day I realized that *of course* these same steps would work for me as I created a new business. I also thought the steps would work for others like me – conscious entrepreneurs who want to shift their business to be more aligned with their emerging passions.

Back to that billboard.

On the day I saw the billboard, I'd had an emotional morning. I watched a brief video of Paul Potts. You might have heard of him. He was a cell phone salesman who thought he was born to do something else.

The video clip began with him talking about how for his whole life he lacked confidence. He took a huge risk and entered "Britain's Got Talent" (sort of like American Idol) to try what he thought he was born to do – sing opera.

I watched the video of his first appearance on that show. As soon as he sang the first few notes, I began to weep. I knew I was weeping because I was watching myself. Only the gender and the dream were different.

There was something I thought I was born to do – share my spiritual knowledge with the world – but I lacked confidence. I was pummeled by fears and questions. "Am I ready? Is this the best direction? Will people reject me if they know about my "woo woo" practices? Do I know enough?

Will anybody pay me to do this? Can I actually make money doing what I love?"

Later that day I saw the billboard. BE YOUR BIG SELF. YOU ARE BEAUTIFUL.

Paul Potts went on to win the competition, and with his prize money, he went to Italy and took singing lessons. He met Pavarotti in the last months of the great tenor's life. Six months after the competition, Paul Potts put out his first CD and launched a concert tour.

And me? Well, once I set the intention to use my soul power to create a business called Soul Power, things started happening. All the help I needed was there. My first paying customers showed up, unsolicited by me, even before I advertised.

Tapping into my soul power has allowed me to create the life of my dreams, and contribute the unique gifts I was born to give the world. Money is flowing in and profits are increasing. Every morning I wake up full of joy. I love helping other conscious entrepreneurs create the lives and businesses their souls yearn for, and give the gifts only they can give the world.

I celebrate and appreciate that my soul gave me a billboard-sized hint.

Tap into *your* soul power.

Bonnie Hutchinson coaches conscious entrepreneurs to create the life and business of their dreams, by tapping into their soul power. Besides being a spiritual junkie, she has a degree in Education and Master's degree in Whole Systems Design. Visit www.soulpowerwisdom.com for a free special report, "Seven Steps to Create a Life of Passion, Purpose and Prosperity: Tapping into Your Soul Power," and a free guided meditation called "Ground and Center."

CHAPTER 24

Benchmarks, Birthdays & Authentic You: Four Principles for Honoring the *You* in Your Business

Janelle J. Jalbert

On the verge of another birthday, I reflected over the last year. The human psyche seems to be intuitively drawn to benchmarking where we are at in relation to where we have been, if not at a birthday then around New Years.

I began my 34th year of life fleeing a toxic teaching position after facing a situation that shook my beliefs, both as a teacher and a person, to my very core. By June, I left for a break from what had become a hellish reality. While in the Frankfurt airport for a layover, I was pulled out of the line and detained. (Who knew English teachers were security risks?) I ended up missing my flight. The day of my return flight via London, the United Kingdom was in the grip of terrorist acts. There was nothing smooth about this trip. That week, I was alone, without luggage, and making it work as I went. I was pushed out of my usual environment, but it ended up being one of the best things that could have happened. Eventually, I gave myself permission to leave a stable paycheck to find out what I really was meant to do, instead of what I believed I ought to do.

By early December, I had begun to hash out a new direction for my life. Then on a Monday in mid-December, my pup, (my substitute child), laid down and couldn't get up. I looked into his fading eyes, said "Good boy" for the last time, and was completely crushed. He had seen me through just about every possible type of crisis: physical, financial, relationship, and employment. He was my unconditional support that everyone needs in order to take a chance. The combination of exploring new avenues and his loss triggered more reflection. I had gotten *Dude,* my dog, more than a decade before as there was a lot of unrest in my heart at that time. That unrest now returned as part of the mourning process. It came from the difference in where I was versus where I deserved to be that continued to be a theme in my life for quite some time.

This difference is the bottom line in why most people strike out on their own. If you ignore the distress, you'll never achieve the success you were meant to achieve. Most entrepreneurs are action oriented in business, but many often overlook the steps to consciously create an authentic, fully integrated life experience. Here are my 4 steps to creating a positive and conscious business and life.

1. Commit to being the star of your life.

The analogy regarding the use of oxygen masks on a plane comes into play here. You put the mask on yourself first because then you then have the ability to help others who are struggling. You can't help others if you yourself are fighting for life. Give yourself permission to get what you need for a happy and healthy life, and then you have a greater ability to assist others.

The next conundrum will be the doubt. If you believed success was possible at any point, then it continues to be possible with enough dedication. Every time doubt enters in, ask yourself truthfully if there is a real basis for it, or if it is simply the fear of the unknown hiding itself in these doubtful feelings. Even if you can't leave your current job immediately to strike out on your own, practice being an entrepreneur in your current position. While acting like an owner in your current role, you are training your mind to view things from a creative, entrepreneurial perspective, and you are becoming a greater service to those around you by honoring your true nature as an entrepreneur. Then, step into the spotlight of your life by just doing it.

2. Define your *life plan* up front.

Notice I did not say business plan, I said *life plan*. In society, we tend to define people by profession. In reality, your profession is a means to enable you to have the greatest life possible. Your job, business, or profession was never meant to be your identity. You work to live, not live to work. Life is far too short to rely on a "lotto" mentality of luck, accident or coincidence. This reinforces the first point. Giving yourself over to the fates is not being the star of your own life story. By giving over or giving up, you are also stopping the proactive flow implied by dependence on "luck" or "coincidence." This is the basis for the law of attraction. You bring into your life that which you are focused on. Don't believe me? For the next two days, notice the number of green cars in town. Or, pick a word you don't hear everyday like "serendipity" and see how quickly someone mentions it in a conversation. Define the life you want, shape your plan to match, and just do it.

3. Cultivate the Push/Pull Principle.

To be more, you have to do more. Find people and experiences that push you beyond your current comfort zone. If you want to be more profitable, find people at that income level. If you want to create your own business, find people who are pursuing their passions. There are countless sayings tied to the idea that "you are judged by the company you keep." It concerns not only the associations you have, but also includes the experiences you pursue. As a parallel, I had always set my sights on being a teacher (complete with embarrassing pictures of me around age 9, teaching my stuffed animals). I never questioned it or checked out my alternatives. As a result, I continued to teach in a variety of settings that led me to experience feelings of spiritual, physical, and emotional distress. It wasn't until I had pushed my passion for travel that I began to envision alternatives.

In thriving through uncertain and unfamiliar experiences, I became the star of my own story. I draw another analogy between my dog Dude and the experience of venturing out to find your authentic self. Dude loved water, but only the natural water that fell from the sky or crashed on the beach. If the word *bath* was even spelled out, he ran for the hills. Inevitably, we would finally get him within a few feet of the bathtub, and he would defiantly plant his rear. We would pull at his collar, and he would somehow think his way to developing a ten-ton butt. Eventually, we would win and he'd get his bath. Afterward, he would run around the house and yard with new vitality. It was the most dreaded, yet best thing ever - once it was finished. Similarly, when we had to put him to sleep, it was the most dreaded, yet best thing ever. In his final months, he was in pain from cancer; we had changed our routines; worried about him before, during, and after our vacations, and I even weighed opportunities on how he might be impacted by the time we spent away. We did everything out of love and without regret. Once Dude was in a better place, it was like I had permission to find a better place for myself. Whether you need to let go of someone or something; find someone to pull you to greater reality; or honor where you have been, give yourself permission to push to the next level and just do it.

4. Honor Your Unique Reality.

Look for connections between seemingly divergent interests, passions, and experiences to find your niche. Every person is here to fulfill a purpose. That purpose is unique to you. No one is neatly summed up in a single word, so you need to see the entirety of what makes you who you are. I'm saying you need to take a supplemental approach to more than just the vitamins you take. You need to understand the variety of interests that spark passion in your life and honor it.

When I looked at my life, I saw teaching as only being represented by what happens in a classroom. I saw community service as something that is "less" important than what brought in the paycheck. I saw my care giving roles as more important than my self-care and so on. I had all these interests, responsibilities and talents that seemed to be all over the place. By getting them down on paper and playing with how I related to them and related them to each other, I was able to define an opportunity that took competing roles and framed them to compliment each other. I have defined a niche that both makes my life more passionate and gives more back to the world than my fragmented and limited perspective allowed before.

Take some time and simply play with your interests to honor your uniqueness and purpose. It's not work; it's play. Give yourself permission to play and just do it.

As a result of these four principles, I sat down to my birthday dinner with a new perspective and vitality regarding the future and a deep gratitude for the experiences I've had. I truly believe to get to the next level, you must step into your spotlight, define your desired reality, push yourself into the new, and honor your uniqueness.

*Janelle works with young adults - focusing on the integration of education, goals, and real-world demands; professionals - seeking assistance in the work/life balance and professional development, and nonprofits – balancing maximization of benefits with profitability. For your **free report** regarding integrating the personal and professional for greater satisfaction and authenticity in life go to www.JCubedLLC.com. To contact Janelle directly for speaking engagements, coaching, or consulting, please email her at JCubedLLC@gmail.com.*

CHAPTER 25

Conscious Communication for Lasting Impact - The Magic of Image and Word

Ankya Klay

I once heard Marija Gimbutas, the Lithuanian archaeologist says: "The images we create shape our world (our collective consciousness). * But perhaps it is also how we chose to match words with the images we create that form our collective consciousness. So what consciousness do we wish to have expressed through us?

Leonard Shlain, (respected author and surgeon at the California Pacific Medical Center in San Francisco) in his book, "The Alphabet Versus the Goddess – The Conflict Between Word and Image," explains that over different periods in history we have shifted between a more masculine linear left brain way of doing, and a feminine circular right brain way of being, according to the dominant influence of the culture at that time (hunters or gatherers). He says that our current extended period of left-brain dominance has come from our learning to write, because to write we have mostly used only our right hand.

He also states that we are now at a unique time in history because of the development of the computer and the World Wide Web (which is inclusive and circular). This is enabling us to 'marry' the analytical left brain with the intuitive right brain. The tool that enables us to do this is the computer. When we work on the computer, we use **both** hands simultaneously so we can connect our right and left brains creatively. When Shlain refers to the Goddess, I believe he means our ability to access our intuitive self. We are shifting our learned ways of operating in a hierarchical competitive system, to a way of being that is a win/win for all.

As conscious entrepreneurs and internet marketers, I believe we have a special place in being part of this shift in global awareness. Not only do we potentially have access to, (and contribute) our awareness and skills to a global market, but we can also help to bridge the gap between mind and heart for our customers. I believe that this is helping bring about a more peaceful world through greater understanding, one person at a time.

As children we were brought up with 'picture' books, and weren't there images everywhere to enhance those wonderful words? Somewhere along the way as we 'grew up', other's led us to believe the idea that it's not 'grown up' to also consider the imagery that is tied to thoughts and feelings.

Yet doesn't an image connect you to your imagination? You most likely have heard the saying "A picture is worth a thousand words." To me this means "A picture's meaning **can express** ten thousand words." This is because an image has a very direct impact on our consciousness and why it is so powerful in accompanying your words. Each person will have their own unique interpretation of an image.

The journey

Life is about change and growth it seems! For many years I worked as a natural therapist, but then about three years ago, spirit had another plan for me. It was calling me in another direction. So I went on a journey - literally and symbolically. I travelled not only geographically, but also went on an inner journey. From this transition period my current business, Ankya Design, 'one earth' images was birthed. Drawing on my holistic awareness, these 'human landscapes' were created for all to enjoy.

Could it be that **we are** the environment? That would mean that how **we** are affects the environment directly. This connection is what I would like to share with you and your customers in my images.

So when you feel those changes tugging at your familiar world, trust that you are on a mysterious journey and follow that thread leading you into your future to be the fullest expression of yourself. It is your heart's 'mind' leading you to a new and creative path for your highest good and the good of all those who come into contact with you.

Follow your intuitive guidance when you 'work.' That is what I am doing right now as I write this chapter for you. I am a vessel and the words are flowing through me for you.

So as a conscious entrepreneur, I invite you to use image and word creatively, in the way you market your business to your customers.

Marrying words with images

To give you an example, one of my most popular images, "water babe," came to me while walking along the beach one day. It's the image of a person's shadow on the sea, and the image triggered this thought. Perhaps we are not as solid as we like to think, but fluid like the element water! Our bodies are mostly made of water aren't they? So maybe that is what connects us to everything and each other. Doesn't water continuously flow through us to be recycled? They say Life all came out of the sea, so perhaps we contain the memory of everything within our cells? So you see an image can inspire a new way of looking and thinking about things.

When it came time to give a title to this image, I listened to the word, (or words) arising from my intuition. The image could have been called any number of things, but the words 'water babe' appeared and I knew that that was to be the title.

How do you know when you have found the right words? Well, perhaps you will get a tingling in your body, or you will feel a resonance, a knowing that **this is it**. This has nothing to do with logic. Maybe you will also experience a sense of joy. That's because you have gotten out of your own way and allowed the experience to come through you. Later perhaps you may think of a more analytical explanation for your choice of words, but it's the initial intuition that is the creative process.

To quote Brad Neuberg, Developer Advocate for Google Gears: "True invention is about channeling something larger than yourself. The muse is that flash of insight that perfectly formed solution that just flashes into your mind." (And I would add from your heart!)

Marrying images to words

So when you want to support your words with an image, relax into a place of surrender and allow the flavor, color or texture of what you want to express to come into your awareness. Then you will receive an intuitive knowing of the kind of image that corresponds and expresses this feeling.

Often we favor one expression over the other – words **or** images. By choosing only one medium we may limit our impact. When you bridge image and word, you expand your potential market and increase the power of your message.

Choosing images

Imagine the symbolic impact of an image. I once had an Indian Feng Shui teacher who had a great suggestion. She said: "When you have a question you have difficulty answering, take yourself off to walk in nature." You will always find a message if you are open to receive, and most likely it will be something quite unexpected. Everywhere in nature there are signs and messages, for instance in the way things relate to one another, or in how they are at different stages of their life cycle.

So, if you are looking for inspiration, or how to express yourself in words or images, stop what you are doing, shift your energy, and step out into nature. Nature is a great teacher. The movement and change of location will shift your energy and allow you to be inspired with fresh impressions. Suddenly the answer will come to you in the shape of a branch, or the placement of a stone. You will experience an 'aha' moment in nature and in that moment you know that you are not alone. You will find the perfect words and image to express what you wish to convey. The whole universe is working with and through you and is ready at each moment to come to your assistance. You no longer need to make it happen, but rather 'allow' it to flow to and through you.

Choosing words

Words are like birds - they each have their own song and unique vibration. Empty your mind, open your heart and you will find the perfect way to express yourself. Just trust your imagination.

When you are designing promotional material for your customers, don't try to be clever, but speak from your heart. Just allow yourself to drop into universal consciousness, and let the appropriate words well up in you to share with them. You may not know what you are looking for, but you will know when you find it! There will be a shift in your energy, and you will just know. This is your reference point. Can you feel your heart sing? If you can, you know you are flowing down the right river.

In closing

When your heart and mind are connected and working together in harmony, **you** are the synthesis of nurturer **and** hunter (the divine feminine and the divine masculine).

So trust your natural ability to allow this process to happen and you will make magic with your images and words to inspire your customers.

Magic is happening now . . .

* The premise of Marija Gimbutas' work on Neolithic prehistory has been summed up in her books, *The Gods and Goddesses of Old Europe*, *The Civilization of The Goddess*, and *The Language of the Goddess*.

Exposed to many cultures, Ankya now lives in Australia. It is her belief that we all walk "one step at a time" on the same mother earth. It is our global connection through Nature that moves her and what she expresses in her images at www. ankya.com. Download her FREE screensaver to inspire your workspace, and meet Blue Bear on his Wild Adventures or visit her site www.ImageYourWorldNow. com. You can contact Ankya via email at hello@ankya.com.

CHAPTER 26

Awakening the Human Spirit: Discovering Purpose and Passion in the Personal Development Industry

Laudi McMullin on behalf of The Freedom Community

Within each of us there exists something unique and powerful. Something intangible that we feel at the deepest level of our being. It is our internal guidance, our soul, our consciousness; it's our passion, our vision and mission in life. That intangible force within us is our human spirit, alive and kicking. It's that powerful energy that never ceases to unfold and is always looking to break through the walls of our conditioned minds and eager hearts. This life force is at every moment calling us towards who we really are and what we really want in life. It is a calling that has led hundreds of conscious entrepreneurs to cross paths and unite in an inspiring and transformative journey.

This is a story of co-creation at its best. It is a story of passion, purpose and collective vision. This is the story of The Freedom Community—a revolutionary group of leading edge visionaries with a heart for helping people.

We begin this story from its inception: a simple yet powerful idea...

An Idea is Born

Many years ago, a brilliant idea was born in the minds of two great men. The idea was to combine personal development with an income opportunity; the goal was to provide ordinary people with a proven path towards personal and financial freedom.

As this idea took root and began growing in its brilliance, something exciting began to happen: the hearts and minds of thousands of ordinary freedom-seeking individuals began lighting up all over North America and several parts of the world as the possibility of financial security and personal fulfillment became a reality for many.

As the international personal development company continued to grow, conscious entrepreneurs from all walks of life gradually found themselves attracted to this path to freedom, choosing to live a life without limits and coming together to co-create greater levels of success through self empowerment programs and a thriving business community. Our Freedom Community was born out of a desire for personal fulfillment, financial freedom, human connection and ongoing collegial support.

Unity in Community

Being business owners working from home can be a fun and exciting experience. It can also be an isolating one for many people. That is why so many of us have opted to unite as a community of entrepreneurs. We each get to benefit from the human connection and continuous growth that comes from sharing our gifts and talents with one another; masterminding around business development; teaching and learning through personal development and financial literacy, and supporting one another in times of need. We have adopted several key success principles which allow us to work on our individual businesses while staying connected to our greater community. The following are only a few of the principles we infuse into our lives and businesses: living and working with integrity and deliberate intention; grounding ourselves in purpose and passion for life; following our own internal guidance at all times; mentoring new business associates to success, and creating personal and financial freedom in our own lives while inspiring others to do the same in theirs.

The heart and soul of our community has grown exponentially over the years as more and more entrepreneurs are drawn to our approach to business and resonate with our mission—to help as many people as possible change the quality of their lives for the better through personal development and financial independence. When inspired entrepreneurs come together and assist one another in being successful, something magical happens: pronounced shifts in collective consciousness take place. These shifts certainly benefit each one of us personally and they also benefit the many people who are influenced by the positive ripple effect of our personal expansion, growth and contagious energy.

Even though all of us were attracted to this community because of our own commitment to freedom, many of us are also committed to the wellbeing and upliftment of others. This is one of the major reasons why collaborating through a professional network is so meaningful. It adds the human touch, the camaraderie and the fun while inspiring greater levels of success within each of us.

A Revolutionary Approach

Most would agree that business tends to be a 'dog-eat-dog' world. And while most business owners are initially focused on their own self-interests, when they are part of our thriving community, they very quickly begin expanding themselves to include the interests of the larger network as well. But why? One might ask. Why would a group of independent business owners collaborate? What makes people trust one another, share resources, support each other and work together? How does that happen?

The answer lies in a radical approach to home-based business. What began as a concept has now evolved into a lively and fully systematized international business network. Our community of entrepreneurs have embraced the company's business apprenticeship model in combination with a 'pay-it-forward' concept, which means that the more people we assist in reaching their personal and financial goals, the more profit we each make. With leading-edge infrastructure and an extensive support system, every new business owner benefits tremendously from the effort and hard work of those who have come before and paved the way. We are all so grateful to be here.

As conscious entrepreneurs we donate our time, our energy and oftentimes our money in order to contribute to our community, simply because we are inspired to do so. Something magical happens when a group of like-minded individuals come together—each one of us here knows exactly what that is. It is our human spirit awakening and breathing once again. It is our human spirit bouncing up and down, eager to play. It's our human spirit in motion, which quickly becomes inspiration in action. And as inspiration moves through each one of us, more and more of that magic grows. And as that magic gets bigger and bigger, those of us who are tapped into the pure positive energy flow reap the benefits of universal gifts manifesting into our experience.

Given that each one of us has been aided and supported by our network in countless ways, it becomes a natural desire to give back to the community that has helped co-create our individual and collective greatness. It becomes the natural extension of who we are each becoming as a result of being a part of this amazing company and inspiring community—*that's* what makes it all work so beautifully.

Discovering Purpose and Passion

Our community operates with an understanding of prosperity consciousness and we are very much dedicated to personal development. Each of us is encouraged to discover our own "why", our deeper reasons for being an entrepreneur. Our "why" becomes the fuel that drives our individual businesses and allows each of us to connect more fully with who we are and what we are each meant to do in this world.

Through our personal development work and the positive culture of our community, many of us have found our own purpose in life and even discovered passions, talents and gifts that we may never have known existed. We are each inspired to grow into our biggest, brightest selves and in doing so, we are able to inspire others to do the same. That inspiration continues to grow and expand while touching people's lives all across the globe, which is such a beautiful thing.

Conscious entrepreneurs in our lively community have chosen to have it all: independence and freedom while enjoying unity in community. Each of us is acutely aware that success depends entirely on our own commitment to freedom. We each understand that creating wealth is a learned skill which takes a great deal of dedication and persistency along with consistent mindset work and an ongoing financial education. We each take full responsibility for our own success and have committed to doing the internal work necessary to create our desired external results. We also realize that while we are the only ones who can make it happen for ourselves, we can have so much more fun along the way when we link arms with those who are on the same path as we are.

Within our hearts, we all know that every human being is born destined for greatness which is why we honor and cultivate personal leadership within our community. We are all inspired to step into our *own* greatness and shine as bright as we were each born to do... the best part is that as we personally grow into our biggest, brightest selves, we also become an inspiration for others to do the same—and *that* is so rewarding.

Something magical happens when conscious entrepreneurs come together... the light within each of us is free to shine as bright as our imagination allows.

The Freedom Community is a group of independent business owners in the field of human potential. They have opted to work in collaboration to use the power of leverage in order to co-create greater levels of success. This win-win model benefits both the individual business owners and their community. As conscious entrepreneurs, they grow personally and financially themselves while assisting others to do the same. For free resources go to www.LeadershipAndAbundance.com.

CHAPTER 27

Wake Up and Smell the Prosperity

Laurel Nevinslong

Just after Christmas in 1993 I was diagnosed with cancer. Although the tumor had invaded the surrounding lymph nodes, it was treatable with surgery and radiation and fourteen years later I am thankful to be alive and healthy. For me the cancer diagnosis was a great big message from the Universe that it was time to **Wake Up And Smell The Coffee.** It was time for me to pay attention and live my life consciously. Thus began my journey of prosperity, although it would take me more than a decade before I would understand this. At the time I just thought of it as a journey of change -- a lot of change.

I left a 14 year relationship that had stopped working several years earlier. I quit my job. I cashed in my 401K and lived off it for several years while I explored what I wanted to do for work. I started to make conscious choices about how I was spending my life's energy, and I began cutting out the energy drains and focusing on the things that really contributed to the quality of my life. I started to listen to my inner guidance and I learned that amazing things happen when you listen.

On New Year's Day 2007, I spent the day with several friends who are artists. They taught me a technique for creating intricate designs with colored wax, metallics and paper. I made a few, but I was more interested in using patterns of words to embellish the ones my friends were making. I had never written poetry before, but as I looked at their unique and remarkable designs, I was compelled to write. Messages about Universal Truth, Spirit and Energy just flowed through me onto the paper. What started out as a crafts project turned into something much more. Three months later these creations were featured at a local art gallery. Sixteen of the pieces sold on the opening night of the show. In just three short months I went from a newbie learning a craft to selling these magical creations.

Around this same time I learned about the Law of Attraction and began to study everything I could find about prosperity consciousness. I studied the work of Abraham-Hicks, Napoleon Hill and many others who teach about harnessing the power of our thoughts to manifest our desires. I learned about connecting to the divine spirit that is in all of us. Plus I learned that true prosperity encompasses all domains of our existence – spiritual, physical, financial, social/emotional and mental.

My favorite definition of prosperity is described by Edwene Gaines in her book "The Four Spiritual Laws of Prosperity: A Simple Guide to Unlimited Abundance." According to Ms. Gaines, true prosperity is:

- "A vitally alive physical body to provide a comfortable worldly home for the spiritual beings that we are."
- "Relationships that are satisfying, nurturing, honest and work all the time."
- "Work that we love so much that it's not work, it's play."
- "And having all the money we can spend."

Since I started actively studying prosperity consciousness and drawing on the fullness of my life experience to make myself open to the prosperity around me, amazing events began unfolding in my life. I've already shared my experience as a burgeoning artist. Here are just a few more of the amazing things that happened over the past year as I am becoming aware of and open to having an abundance of prosperity in my life:

- Having never flown first class, the airline upgraded my seats twice in the last six months.
- One week after I decided I needed a commuter car, a friend emailed me

asking if I knew of anyone who could use the car she was ready to pass on to a new owner.

- An unexpected check for $5000 arrived the very day after I discovered a deficit of several thousand dollars in my cash flow for that month.
- In one year I went from being more than $40,000 in debt, to being debt free.
- At my current job, my program budget was unexpectedly doubled and our center was given $100,000 of unsolicited additional funding.
- After spending months meditating on manifesting a million dollars, I was stunned to discover that as administrator of my late aunt's estate, I have responsibility for more than one and a half million dollars that, prior to her death, the family had no idea existed.

These are but a few examples of the prosperity that is manifesting in my life now. I am cultivating a prosperity consciousness and I practice having a prosperous mindset on a daily basis. As part of my own journey of prosperity, I gathered hundreds of pages of writings and resources from centuries of teachings on the topic. From those writings I have extracted seven essential steps to prosperity that have guided me on my journey and that I now wish to share with you.

1. Wake up and be conscious.

In this fast paced world, we too often get consumed with 'doing,' caught up in the many activities that make up modern life. Our days are filled with appointments, commitments and activities. We're so busy 'doing' that we forget about 'being.' The first step to prosperity is to s-l-o-w down, to be mindful and conscious – awake and aware.

2. Clear the clutter.

Our mental and physical worlds are filled with stuff. All of that stuff consumes energy; energy to maintain it, store it, even just to have it around. Getting rid of clutter in our physical environment frees up energy and makes room for other things to come into our lives. Clearing mental clutter is equally important. As Nick Nolte's character says in the movie *Peaceful Warrior*, "Throw out the trash."

3. Cultivate a prosperous mindset.

Clearing out the mental clutter - emptying out the negative self-talk and limiting beliefs - makes room to develop a prosperous mindset. Do I think like a poor person or do I think like a prosperous person? Do I assume that good things are going to happen to me or bad things? Our prosperity mindset is reflected in everything that we think and say, from the smallest things, like finding a parking space on a busy street, to the fulfillment of our biggest dreams.

4. Live with purpose.

Focus on being who we came here to be. By remembering that we are spiritual beings having a human experience rather than a human being having a spiritual experience, we remain connected to our divine purpose.

5. Tap the power of thoughts.

Students of the Law of Attraction understand the power our thoughts have to create our experience. Simply stated, like attracts like, and what we think about becomes reality. Wayne Dyer captured this concisely in the title of his recent book "Change Your Thoughts - Change Your Life." To be truly prosperous we need to be visionaries, believing wholeheartedly in our visions, and not allowing ourselves to remain stuck in what "is."

6. Be a good receiver.

I used to be a terrible receiver. All too often when surprised with a present, I would find myself saying "You shouldn't have" or "I can't accept this." Later I realized that the message I was sending was "Don't give me any good stuff." Being a good receiver sends a powerful message to the Universe that we willingly and joyfully accept all that is in store for us. We are open to all of the prosperity that the Universe has to offer.

7. Live with gratitude.

I recently heard a radio interview that reminded me of the power of living with gratitude. John Scripter was the first person to undergo a heart transplant at a world renowned hospital in Boston. After the historic operation, the doctors told the Scripter family that John might live for five years. After John's death, his wife Linda told interviewers of the tremendous gratitude that her husband felt for the additional time he was given. He greeted each day with thanks and appreciation. John Scripter has been called a "miracle man" living for twenty-two years following the heart transplant; twice as long as the average heart transplant recipient.

We can all follow John Scripter's example and live with gratitude and appreciation for the abundance and prosperity that exists in each and every day. Be conscious and aware of the abundance that surrounds us. Make room for good things to come into our lives. Clear out the negative beliefs and tap the power of our thoughts to create the things we desire to experience.

This is the journey of prosperity and it is the journey of the conscious entrepreneur. Central to prosperity and conscious business are a commitment to following one's inner guidance, a willingness to fulfill one's divine plan, and making a difference in the world.

Don't wait for the Universe to send you a big nasty cosmic wake up message. Wake up and smell the Prosperity. Be conscious. Be entrepreneurial. Be prosperous. It is your birthright.

For over 20 years Laurel has used her unique talents for researching, analyzing, synthesizing and sharing information in a wide array of nonprofit, private sector and public sector endeavors. A lifelong learner and an avid teacher, Laurel created the Conscious Prosperity Circle – an online community and resource center promoting the transformation of prosperity consciousness worldwide. Download the free special report, "Prosperity is Your Birthright, Claim It Now" at www.ConsciousProsperityCircle.com. Email her at Laurel@ConsciousProsperityCircle.com, Telephone: 781.308.3906.

CHAPTER 28

Wake up Wondering, Not Worrying

Kelley Rexroad

The role of entrepreneur can be just another role, and it can be thrust upon us by the circumstances of the moment. This role can be something that occurs without much thought or planning. It can be a rebound love from a corporate job; an old dream; an agreement after a football weekend or even a family forced future.

Without thought an entrepreneur can just add to an already lengthy to do list. We stay busy to buy things we need or think we need. If we stay busy we can have "this thing" and then be happy.

We set ourselves up to fail.

We set up elaborate goal systems around activity not meaningful results. There are systems around color-coding, numbering, alphanumeric and even paper or electronic or both! Do these renew our commitment to achieve goals? Within days, the system becomes a disarray of sticky notes, magazine articles, clippings and business cards. Goals are just another thing to do after collapsing at the end of the day, depleted from diffused energy. Even a water pitcher must be filled to keep pouring from it and so we must work to restore our energy.

Three little words

An entrepreneur can find energy by changing the order of three words: be, do and have.

Being

"What do you want to be when you grow up?" was a common childhood question. Did you answer, "Tired, worn out, on the road, but grateful that I at least have benefits." Or did you answer. "I want to be stuck in a position because of an obligation." That is not a wonderful way to be. Thank goodness, children are blue-sky in their thinking. Potential cowboys, teachers, astronauts, doctors, race car drivers and firemen, or as several of my nephews wanted to be - a garbage man - were never troubled with how to pay for schooling or what others think of their dreams. As a child, no paperweight etched with, "What would you do if money was no object?" was needed when dress up was played and dreams were made. It was about the dream, the passion and the EXCITEMENT of being.

Somehow along the way, we burdened ourselves with things, the need to impress and boxes of stuff. Our life became filled with places to go and people to meet, and more things to buy. Our success somehow was caught up in the success of those things owned by others. The act of 'doing' rather than 'being' took on a life of its own complete with the gadgets to fill the time. No more conversations in the car, quiet moments at the beach or talks about what to watch together on television. We plan the next activity, and forget to take in the experience. We don't even have the memory of the moment we are "doing."

The doing - the busyness, the activity - all took over. It filled time up. A wise editor once said to me, that when everything is bold, nothing is bold. What can possibly be important when everything is considered urgent? What time is left to determine importance?

The schedules of children, the soccer game, traveling league, dance, tutor and all of the events have lead us to wondering what to say when there is quiet time. How do we just be? What is the value of the still time? So much of our quiet times are spent worrying—"How will I make payroll? Pay for insurance? Make this or that happen? How will I get it all done?"

Now does this mean that entrepreneurism is just pondering the wonders of life or examining our own belly button? Of course not. Being instills passion. It is about staying focused on the goals, not the tasks. It is the movement of the business, in its every changing form and heights and depths. It is the movement within us as we rediscover and reach the blue sky.

So, if being an entrepreneur is just simply 'being', how is that state obtained? That's the beauty of it. You can start now. You can consciously choose by deciding what you want at this very moment. You can choose not to react, but choose your intention. What will you do today to be that successful business owner? Will you complete the paperwork you hate? Will you make the cold calls to fill the pipeline of work? Can you start with ten minutes?

Do to be

If your decision to be an entrepreneur was only to accumulate "more stuff" –when will you have enough? Are you powerless over your addiction to more things, to a title, a role, or a flashy car? If you wanted flexibility to help you be a better father, rather than be a father over a few vacation weeks a year, then today make a choice to go to that ball game. Today read the story at bedtime. Today share prayers with your child.

Perhaps the doing of being a spouse gets sucked up in doing the laundry, preparing the dinner, getting the oil changed and the lawn work completed. To be a good spouse may mean being able to choose to do something nice at your next opportunity, not just on a special occasion. Stop what are you doing when she/he comes home and look into their eyes. Take a bit more time in that moment of a hello kiss. I remember that my Dad always kissed my mom goodbye. Today, I realize that it is part of my being a loving spouse. Sit next to your beau on the couch tonight and hold hands during the TV show. Being a better spouse means being the role, not acting it, and not filling all available free time with activities. Make the memory by experiencing it.

Have you reached out to your community? How will you be more civic minded in your business role? Will you volunteer a day of your time or take an hour to give blood today? Or will you be a volunteer to Habitat for Humanity sometime in the future? Take that list of 'to do' items and decide today what you want to be as an entrepreneur and a citizen in your community.

When your passion, energy and excitement are behind your work, it is not a four-letter word anymore. It becomes a joy. It is ideas and energy. It is also the peace that comes from knowing that the tiredness you feel is from a burning cycle of ideas which come so fast that you can not share them, as the next idea is in your head before you can describe the current thought. You are building something. You are organizing and are systemizing your business. You are being the 5 year old child filled with wonderment except you now have the experience and maturity framework. You are smart enough to know that you may need help along the way.

The haves will come

For when you are being an entrepreneur and you choose each day to do what is meaningful for you, the passion drives you to the third word—'have.' The contacts you need and the opportunities you want will show up. You just "need to get out of your own way," as my Granny said. When you can have the ability to buy all the 'stuff' you wanted and the things you thought you needed, it is then when a new sense of being comes over you. Dorothy, in the Land of Oz with her red shoes, always knew it was there. It is the being, creating and the ability to share and give that multiplies our well-being, and at a much greater rate than depreciation of the latest electronic gadget or car. 'Stuff' doesn't make us happy.

The peace you find because you have been able to be a better business person, a better spouse and/or a better neighbor allows you to know that what you have given to others has been returned a hundredfold. You have set a positive example, not written about the ten steps to better parenthood, but by being it each day. What is one thing you can do today to be that person you want to be?

To be awakened is fine, but to actually 'do' is still necessary.

Being a conscious entrepreneur means making a fully conscious choice each and every time. The entire day gives us multiple opportunities to say a nicer word, use a better tone, and have a bit more patience. There is a difference between worry lines and laugh lines, so make a choice to have more of the latter.

Consider this: How would your business be if you were simply being you and didn't take yourself quite so seriously? Get out of your own way and let yourself be the person you are deep inside. Wake up each day wondering, "What opportunities will present themselves today? Who will I meet?" The ripple effect you send by what you do will change the world, your business, your family and yourself.

Welcome to the business of 'being.'

America's HR Strategist™, Kelley Rexroad grew up in a family business, and worked 25 years in corporate communications and global human resources. She is a nationally published author and speaker and was recognized as a finalist for the Tampa Bay Business Woman of the Year. Kelley consults with organizations and coaches successful people who want a richer life of success. Reach her at kelley@krexconsulting.com or 813-920-9030. Her website is www.krexconsulting.com.

CHAPTER 29

7 Steps to Raise the Bar to Genius Level in Your Business and Life That You Can Begin Right Now

Cathy Silva

As someone with Entrepreneurial Spirit, you *require* freedom and flexibility to be at your best. You need space to create. Yet the busyness of your life and business can stifle your creativity and entrap you in a script that's not your own. You soon realize that your business is running your life, and not the other way around.

Seven years ago when I started my business, Innerwiz Coach, I thought, "This is it. This is my purpose. This is what I was born to do." I experienced pretty quick success, but then became overwhelmed by the busyness of my life and business. Like you, Business Owner was just one of my many roles. It was a struggle to accomplish it all.

The voice from within kept repeating "Clear the decks." I just needed some space; to breathe, to create, and just be.

When you make a plea from your heart to God, know that God is ready and willing to deliver whatever you truly desire. And if *you* do what you need to do to turn things around, one way or another that which you desire will come to you.

So, one by one, each of my clients stopped working with me. *Then*, I had the space I needed.

Trust me, the Universe is conspiring with you to co-create whatever your heart desires.

Wayne Dyer writes in *Sacred Self*, "Intelligence flows through everything in the universe and has had many names. It causes the planets to orbit, the galaxies to stay in place, the seedlings to sprout, the flowers to open and you, yes you, to breathe and walk and think."

You were created from this 'Intelligence, God, Universe' - (whatever you choose to name it). I call it God *and* know it as *pure genius*. If you could see yourself and the world from God's perspective, you would see perfection, balance, and genius! You have within you the gifts, talents, and natural instincts necessary to successfully grow the business you desire. You do!

You have a mission as unique as your fingerprint. Your business is simply *your* unique mission and message in action.

In order for Innerwiz Coach to be my unique mission, fully expressed I had to make some adjustments in my thinking and in my daily actions. I had to regain consciousness as it were; to be willing to *be* in business in a *whole new way*. The purpose of this book is to show you a new way to *be* in business. I promise you that by fully embracing and implementing the ideas and strategies I am sharing with you; your life, business and the world will be transformed.

As your coach and guide along this new journey, my passionate mission is to inspire and empower your *inner genius*. I will be your personal guide through the essential steps that will take you out of the busyness and chaos of your life and put you firmly on your sacred path to success.

As we journey together you will see that your level of success is not as much determined by external matters or accomplishments such as degrees or work experience, but has more to do with inner matters of the spirit. There are universal principles which when applied to your everyday life, will allow your life and business to unfold *beautifully, naturally, and perfectly*.

So let's begin...

Your Inspired Vision

There is an invisible energy that comes from within that naturally pulls you forward and guides you. Your "Vision" comes from this energy. It differs from a "goal." 'Setting a goal' creates resistance, especially if it's not the right goal for you, and it requires that you push forward to attain that goal. Your vision comes from that place within where everything is possible. When you are fully present to what you truly desire, it naturally pulls you forward and compels you to act accordingly. Allow your vision to be *really good, outrageous, and magnificent*. Use all your senses. Use detail and 'color' to envision the whole picture. How does your business fit with all the areas of your life – your family, relationships, and leisure? *Pause here to do this before you go on.*

Grounding Your Vision

Now, wasn't that fun? How did it feel to really let your imagination run wild? Does it kind of feel like a fantasy? If you stopped at this point and dismissed it all as another "impossible dream", that's just what it would be – an impossible fantastic dream; a fantasy.

Let's assume, however that you've drawn that line in the sand; you've made the decision to create a business that makes you wealthy and makes a difference in the world. Let's bring that vision of yours to real life! Here is where you begin to play and create from *your* natural genius. We're going to create a 'visual' image here. You might want to use a special journal for the distinct purpose of writing down your vision and inspirations as they come to you. I suggest you use a journal without lines, as that way you have more of an open space to play with. When you write, use present tense language that states that what you desire already exists. For example, "I am so happy and grateful now that I've gained 30 new clients who are a joy to work with and pay me well". Is your inner Picasso dying to come out and play? If so, draw or paint your inspired vision, or create your work using both words *and* pictures. Have fun with it! Express yourself anyway you desire. It's *your* dream and *your* genius! When your masterpiece is complete, share it with someone. Sharing it makes it more real too!

Gather an "Inner Circle of Support"

It's vital to the safety and freedom of your genius to have unconditional love and support as your business grows. Be sure to enroll your spouse, family, and friends in the process. Tell them what you are up to and how they can help. For example, while I write this chapter, my friends and family know I am not available for our lively long chats on the phone. And my husband is taking up the slack around the house. I am blessed with this vital support *because* I have communicated my commitment to my mission while honoring the needs and values of others. It's a beautifully balanced exchange of love and everyone wins!

Clearing the Clutter

That nagging voice in my head "to clear the decks" was the result of having way too much 'stuff' that wasn't serving the business I wanted to create.

Your next step is to clear some space for yourself. Examine your living and work space, relationships, and family. What distracts you? What drains your energy? What keeps you from enjoying people and life? Where is there chaos or challenge? What can you take off that 'to do list' by delegating or dumping it? It's amazing what we as humans put up with without even being aware of it. Make a new list of 'clutter items' that you can begin addressing now.

Treasure Hunting

The treasure we seek is within you. It is all the aspects of your particular genius - your gifts, talents, natural instincts, personality, and core values. Once you have identified and embraced the aspects of you that perfectly equip you for *your* unique mission, you begin to feel a sense of connection and flow. You more clearly prioritize projects and actions- and know what is a definite "Yes" and an absolute "No". You are "tapped in" to the universal flow; GOD = Genius!

Life Environments

When I'm working with clients, we look at *seven life environments*: spiritual, physical, financial, social, family, work, and relationship. You might have realized by now that this is not just about your business. It's about creating a beautifully balanced life! Once you have cleared the clutter, and identified your core gifts and values, you can custom design these key life environments to support your natural work flow, effectiveness and creativity. A good place to start is with the physical environment of your home office. Clean out a closet or file drawer. Purge the old and clear a space to create a space that inspires you.

Attraction in Action

The Law of Attraction states that the right people, resources, and opportunities you seek are seeking you. However, tapping into this universal law does require action - daily conscious, consistent, high priority action. You are now more awake to the genius within you. You are more aware of what you were born to do. Choose your actions wisely. Delegate those things that are someone else's best work and that are getting in the way of *your* genius work. Most of all, remember to play and enjoy what comes to you!

Cathy Silva is the founder of Innerwiz Coach, through which she lives her mission to 'instigate and inspire the genius within.' Cathy is the creator of **Holy Groundwork**, *A Discovery and Development Process That Brings the Brilliance of Who You Are Out Into the World to Make a Difference and Experience True Success. Visit www.Innerwiz.com for the free expanded 7 Steps to Raise the Bar to Genius Level In Your Life and Business.*

CHAPTER 30

Your Business as Your Calling to Serve the World: Your spiritual wisdom and intuition + practical applications = inner peace, harmony and joy.

Gloria Tom Wing Staudt

As an inspirational success coach for peak performing entrepreneurs, I've learned a few secrets I'd like to share with you. You see, I believe you were born to be extraordinarily successful... while enjoying a deep sense of fulfillment, peace, harmony and joy. Conscious entrepreneurship is the journey of a lifetime that will encourage you to grow, expand, release, heal, renew and be your authentic, radiant self. To guide you along your journey, I'd like to share my seven principles for thriving as a conscious entrepreneur.

Clarify Your Vision

Are there days when your business is not going the way you want, doubts creep in, others reaffirm your doubts and you forget that it is your calling to serve the world? Do you compare yourself with others and ignore your intuition to trust your unique way of making a difference in the world through your business? If you've answered yes to these questions, this is a reminder for you to connect with your vision and to use spiritual wisdom to guide you daily.

Most likely you have a deep knowing that you are on your divine path. And, when you are "in the flow" and living your vision, you have inner peace and harmony, feel at ease in your daily actions, happy about your relationships, make a difference in the world and attract new customers easily. This is what it's like when you connect with, and express, your soul's passion and purpose. Naturally, prosperity follows in surprising ways which you consciously appreciate.

When you live according to your highest vision, your soul's passion and purpose are authentically expressed. And when you are authentic, you radiate peace, harmony and joy and inspire others. You feel on purpose with your business and your life is soul satisfying, because when you express who you really are in your most natural and easy way, your soul sings and you profoundly affect others by being and doing what you love. Your vision must guide you on a loving journey that inspires integrity in all areas of business and life.

Stay Awake on Your Journey

Along your entrepreneurial journey, you've likely discovered that when you are living your vision and doing work you love, you feel joy, time passes easily, and there is a natural feel to what you do and it doesn't feel like 'work' at all. Chances are you can recall how much of a journey it was to simply arrive at the decision to commit to your business and life vision. Until you do that, your journey is a completely different one.

Before you committed to staying awake on your journey, you may have seen opportunities as obstacles, or compromised your intuition to make a quick decision you hoped would move you forward. Many of my clients express feeling alone with their thoughts prior to working with me. You may feel the same way if you don't have the right support systems around you.

When you're awake on your journey, you evolve differently than those around you. Other people, who don't understand your journey, may express their fear about your decision and not support you in your entrepreneurial pursuits. Yet, you cannot be pulled off track because of your deep knowing that you are destined to pursue your business. Somewhere along your journey, you became open to learning and completely aware of how empowering it was to shift your perspectives and experience dramatically different results. These are the gifts of staying awake on your journey.

Present is perfect

Your first response may be that nothing is perfect. However, when you see the present moment as perfect you will have no stress. Usually during a challenging time, your thoughts are of past mistakes, or future anticipation of mistakes, which leads to a present moment feeling of stress in your body. What if you see the present as perfect in the moment, acknowledge what is, feel deep appreciation for all your blessings, connect with your heart and soul's desires and intentions and make a choice from that place? Can you see how you will have no stress in that moment?

Every challenge is an opportunity bearing gifts of inspiration

Often, a challenge or problem equals stress until you find a solution or the problem goes away. However, from a conscious perspective, when you view a challenge or problem as an opportunity bearing gifts of inspiration, this lets you tap into your creativity by looking for an outcome that will improve yourself, your business and your relationships. You then powerfully choose where to focus your mind's attention and authentically make heart and soul centered decisions. Consequently, stress is minimized and your conscious choices lead to rewarding results which at times are not what you had expected.

Everything happens for the highest good of all

You may question this and find embracing it will require some practice. However, by choosing this perspective, you focus your attention on looking for the opportunities or gifts of the situation, and are not distracted by what is neither useful nor helpful to all concerned. You connect with who you really are and with your purest of intentions. You take action from that pure place and you surrender to a higher power.

Trust your intuition

Belief in a higher source, God, the universe or however you describe it, is your most powerful tool. Some describe your intuition as God speaking to you. By trusting your intuition, 'gut' sense or hunch, you will not be led astray. You have this ability which can be developed the more you trust it. You may ask, how you will know if it is your intuition or something else? Your intuition has no hidden agendas and wants only what is best for you in the purest sense; it is not your mind rationalizing or your emotions revealing. Your intuition aligns with your heart mind and soul as your divine guidance.

Be of service to one another

Your passion and purpose means you are to serve yourself, as well as be of service to others with your talents. Serving yourself may feel like a selfish thing to you. However, this care of self, physically, emotionally, intellectually and spiritually, means you have the best to give in serving others. As a conscious entrepreneur, you know that your business reflects a marriage of your skills, talents and service to one another, in making a difference in the world. Everyone wins doing business with you.

How This All Works

To help you practice the above principles (which requires a lot of courage) I'd like to share some of my client's experiences in putting these into action. I share their stories in the hope that you will see a part of yourself in them, and that they'll help you find the courage to transform your life and business.

Interior Designer, Daine, (www.cometinteriordesign.com) *followed her intuition* despite fears of the unknown to commit fully to a business which expresses her passion, skills and talents. She explored what was unfamiliar; handled her needs, and lives a value based life. She continually invested in personal and business development, and discovered creative ways of doing business to shine more brilliantly. As a result, she naturally attracted more of her ideal customers. Are you ready to face the unknown, honor your *intuition* and be an inspiration to your customers?

Image consultant and opera singer, Lilly, (www.flairimage.ca) knew at an early age that she loved makeup and had a natural flair in her personality and the way she dressed. After 2 successful careers, she *followed her vision* and moved in the direction of her desire. She was persistent, honored her priorities and experienced a more rewarding life. Lilly was determined to enjoy and appreciate her life, hold on to the vision of her business despite obstacles along the way, and also attracted more business with every step she took to move forward. Are you ready, to enjoy peace and fulfillment resulting from making the commitment to live your *vision*?

Opera singer and voice teacher, Mary Anne, (www.maryannebarcellona. com) has a deep faith in God, an amazing gift of her voice and a desire to continue to use her talents to *be of service to others*. She continually explores new ways of developing herself and is determined to help others live a life of beauty, peace and harmony. Her courage and determination to take extremely great care of herself, and answer her call to fully express her talents in her business, allows Mary Anne to enjoy a meaningful life that serves others. Do you have a deep yearning to express your talents while *touching the lives of others*?

Something To Think About

Take some time now to answer the following questions. They'll help you implement these seven principles into your business and your life:

1) What is the vision of yourself and your business? 2) Are you authentically expressing yourself daily? 3) Does your business reflect your passion and purpose? 4) What is missing to balance your life and business? 5) Who is on your support team? 6) Are all aspects of your heart, mind and soul's environment on track to keep you inspired?

Gloria Tom Wing Staudt is an inspirational success coach and an enthusiastic leader of an award winning Burnaby Metrotown Rotary Club. As an entrepreneur, she makes a significant difference in people's lives by using practical applications of spiritual wisdom for successful results. Through her

business, she provides coaching and assessment services via the telephone, internet and in person. Request a free copy of "Secrets to Inner Peace, Harmony & Joy" at www.PeakSuccessCoaching.com or email Gloria@ PeakSuccessCoaching.com.

CHAPTER 31

The "IS Fac^tor" – A Conscious Strategy to Achieving Your Bottom Line©

Yarrow

So You Want to "Be" a Conscious Entrepreneur!

Great news! Fortunately, you come equipped with a significant innate quality - a desire to make a difference.

Conscious entrepreneurship is really simple...it's just not easy. Consciousness, simply defined, is a state of engaging in personal accountability and personal responsibility. The concept is being aware of any messes (deliberate or not) that you make, and take personal responsibility to clean them up. And, it is really simple; however, it takes persistent mindfulness i.e. being conscious of your thoughts and actions.

Being a conscious entrepreneur involves making choices that originate from your spirit, your true essence - that part of you that knows you have something of value to share. Consciousness is a holistic lifestyle involving the body, mind and spirit where, each moment, your actions and behavior are tangible results of what you think. Your essential values and your highest expression are key to designing a purpose-driven business and a soul-satisfying life.

Perhaps like most people, all you want is to be loved and accepted. It is through expressing your unique talents that you can best serve humanity. When you live from the "right action of your heart," you exude an uplifting energy of happiness and abundance. This is your state of "being" or rather how you show up in the world and how others perceive you. Your uniqueness is expressed through the essence of your energy. This is what I refer to as the "IS Fac^tor."

Integrating a Conscious Operating Procedure (COP) – A Soul-Satisfying Standard for a Conscious Entrepreneur

Most businesses operate from a strategic plan that supports their mission and includes Standard Operating Procedures (SOP) designed to maneuver the leaders toward accomplishment of a predetermined bottom line.

In the SOP model, many individuals and their ideas are ousted along the way if they do not fully buy into what the company wants to accomplish. Thinking outside the normal company culture and being the voice of change is not always beneficial. Within this unconscious SOP business model, people often do not feel respected, appreciated and honored. As a result, the bottom line is frequently fraught with low performance, high turnover and a feeling of dissatisfaction.

When you choose to integrate Conscious Operating Procedures (COP) as your business standard, you bring a new energy and spirit of consciousness to your life through communications, negotiations, solutions and actions that result in mutual outcomes. Strategies are implemented through authenticity, integrity and compassion; responses are appropriate for any given situation, regardless of the outcome.

Here's an example of conscious communication: When engaged in discussion set aside previous conversation. Seek to listen with presence and integrity and not be swayed by thoughts such as, "Here we go again."

When you choose to live a COP lifestyle, your business and life are guided by the principle of "for the higher good of all, with the potential for the least harm."

Since your actions are a direct result of your thoughts, you are now showing up in your life with a spirit of consciousness that saturates your life with meaning and purpose. You are creating a new you – a conscious entrepreneur!

Why Be a Conscious Entrepreneur?

A lifestyle of consciousness is a choice. It requires purposeful thought and action. When you align yourself in your thinking, doing and being, you achieve the rewards of passion and a deeper connection to your higher self. A clearer sense of purpose and greater meaning in your life transpires. You are "being" the "IS Fac^tor." And, your motto is "How can I better serve?"

Here's an example of conscious thinking: To better serve, your ego cannot be in control of your mind. Your mantra is, "Client first and mission oriented."

Pioneers are courageous, undaunted individuals who carry the energy of "change agents." Passion fuels their vision; they wave the flag of new concepts, heralding in what appears to be radical ways of thinking. In corporate America, pioneers and their ideas are often ostracized. In certain business settings, some may call them visionaries; others refer to them and their thinking as dangerous, half-cooked and extreme.

As an entrepreneur, you have purpose and a vision. You are also empowered with a consciousness to design the characteristics of your unique "IS Fac^tor" simply by your choices. You can choose to be open for and accepting of what shows up; you can choose to have a compassionate heart; and you can choose to be a conscious vehicle for receiving and giving back. Through this re-engineering of your thinking, you are choosing to "be" a conscious entrepreneur, a beginning strategy to achieve your bottom line.

The information that follows informs you about "what is" in any situation. These tools illustrate the successful impact you can have with your clients and impart strategies on ways to achieve a mutual bottom line. Again, it is simple, just not easy. This information supports you in developing and "being" your unique "IS Fac^tor." (Visit www.ConciousToolbox.com to download your free *"IS Fac^tor" Conscious Entrepreneur Strategy Checklist.*)

The "IS Fac^tor" - What is "IS?"

You may have heard the term, "It just is." Much of life shows up as situations you cannot control, replete with people who have differing opinions from yours. For instance, a business culture or environment *is* the cultural "IS Fac^tor" and is often distressed by obstacles and challenges. Regardless, individuals are expected to succeed.

Perhaps the cultural "IS Fac^tor" shows up as a leader reluctant or ill-equipped to provide inspired leadership; a colleague focused on sabotaging others who possess credible ideas and solid work ethics; or a manager comfortable with the status quo. This "just is" the cultural "IS Fac^tor."

You may recognize the "IS Fac^tor" as something you find absurd, frustrating, unthinkable, unrealistic, unreasonable, unfair and so on. Nonetheless, you can agree to define it as it "just is" and free up the time and energy you use thinking that you can change it. Then refunction that energy to support your intention of creating a purpose-driven business and soul-satisfying life.

The challenge within the cultural "IS" becomes a shared one. Your mission is to create a COP complete with strategies anticipated to achieve a mutual bottom line.

Creating Your Unique "IS Fac^tor."

The openness to receive new information and the willingness to embrace change are two critical components to becoming a conscious entrepreneur. These characteristics along with your skills, talents, truth and experience are not the only tools needed to accomplish mutual goals with your clients. Your conscious entrepreneur thinking and how you approach clients and the business cultural is your unique "IS Fac^tor." Practice these revolutionary strategies to develop and define your own unique "IS Fac^tor":

- RE-train your thoughts – Embrace the "IS Fac^tor" to create inspired solutions and achieve mutual bottom-line goals;
- RE-think your choices – Choose to do the right thing! Eliminate the blame factor;
- RE-language your words and concepts – Empower others through active listening, authentic understanding, and honest communication;
- RE-design your responses – Be mindful of the cultural "IS Fac^tor";
- RE-function your energy – Focus on how you can make a difference in any situation.

Tools to Foster Your Personal "IS Fac^tor."

You are likely ready to enjoy the benefits of being a conscious entrepreneur -- purpose, passion and profits. Store the following three tools in your "conscious toolbox" and retrieve them to make a difference:

1. Eliminate procrastination – take care of the small stuff before it escalates to a crisis;

2. Be mentally active instead of mentally passive – "be" the change you want to see;

3. Resist trying to change people and situations – re-function your energy to support positive outcomes.

Living the "IS Fac^tor."

During your time here in this *earth school*, you have the unique opportunity to live your purpose and share your passion, giving others the courage to also live a purpose-driven business and soul-satisfying life.

"Being" the "IS Fac^tor" is similar to the concept of "letting your light shine" so others can also find their way to enlightenment and awareness.

Awareness is thought by many as being irreversible. As Fred Kofman explains in his book *Conscious Business*, "Shamans warn that you should meet knowledge with the impeccable spirit of a warrior, ready to face death: death understood not as a physical demise, but as the loss of old familiarities and relationships."

You can start "being" the "IS Fac^tor" and consciously create your purpose-driven business and soul-satisfying life by integrating these conscious strategies into the way you "be":

- Surrender to what "just is" as the starting point of your interactions;
- Engage in credible responsibility;
- Resolve any unfinished business immediately;
- Recognize and value other perspectives;
- Know that the journey to achieving the bottom line is enhanced by the spirit of how you are "being."

As you live and "be" the "IS Fac^tor", enjoy achieving your bottom line in both your purpose-driven business and your soul-satisfying life...AND expect your life to show up differently!

Yarrow is skilled in communicating cutting-edge concepts and engages individuals and groups in embracing change by entertaining contemporary paradigms. She is inspired to bring hope to those seeking more out of life through motivational lectures, education and personal development tools. Schedule Yarrow to help bridge the gap between your unconscious routine and the "IS Fac^tor" of your conscious reality. www.ConsciousToolbox.com or 410.271.1377. FREE ~ Retrieve your "IS Fac^tor" Conscious Entrepreneur Strategy Checklist at www.ConsciousToolbox.com.

PART III:

Thriving in
Your Ultimate Business

CHAPTER 32

The Secret Blueprint To Creating Your FABULOUS Business, Even If You're Now Starting Out Or You're Just Starting Over!

Sandra Baptist

"Finally! It is my time to shine! Finally! I can live my own life and run my own business as I know I can! Thank you!"

If you're an aspiring professional or solo-entrepreneur, I'm sure you too were saying the same things, only to say, not less than a few months later "Great Senses, what was I thinking?"

Well, like you, no less than 17 months after starting my business I did indeed realize that this was not what I had in mind.

I wanted Freedom. Time freedom, financial freedom, stress freedom, employee-drama freedom. I was tired of the less-than-ideal clients. I was not into the competition back-biting, the 'white-lies' and rumor-spreading mill simply to gain an extra buck. I was sick of not having fun!

I knew if I wanted the life I had envisioned, something would have to change -and change soon.

I remembered some years ago I had created a step-by-step process that took into account the important strategies for literally attracting the business of your dreams...a business where you could play more and make more.

Yikes! This is exactly what I needed right now to get my business back on track. Isn't it wonderful how we always get the answers when we ask the right questions?

I dug up this system, this blueprint from my old laptop, and began to fine tune it, tweak it and use it in my own business and it worked!

What was good about this system is that it helped me to see that there is truly no competition within the service-based industry (after all, there is only one YOU).

By becoming more aware of our own power and of our own ability to create remarkable businesses, we begin to unconsciously create them through our daily actions and the decisions we make.

Okay, so let me tell you what you need to get clear on, in order to become the proud owner of a FABULOUS business - one where the business owner is authentic while still making money and profit. Gosh is this even possible, you might ask?

Yes! The very first thing you need to do is to **Figure out where you want to be in 3 years.** This is not your normal business plan for the bank, with your carefully- worded executive summary and 12-month cash flow projections. I'm talking here about focusing on creating a powerful 3-year vision for your business. A vision whose excitement will keep you focused.

A cluttered mind is a confused mind, I dare say, and sadly it'll keep your business from going forward in leaps and bounds.

And that's just the tip of the iceberg! I know of service professionals that tell their clients what they're going to do, how they will do it and what their service costs will be too early in the initial meeting stages. B-o-r-i-n-g. Facts tell, but stories sell, don't you agree?

Activate your creative juices and tell your customers your story. Put it everywhere. On your marketing materials, website, car decal etc.

We, (the buying public) want to know what you did and how you did it. We need to feel a connection with you to purchase your services and by creating this connection, you may end up with a customer for life.

What's the lifetime value of one client to you? Thousands or hundreds of thousands of dollars?

Sounds great, huh?

But let me tell you how you can really attract some 'sticky' customers.

Brand yourself by determining what differentiates you from other businesses. This is your road to gold, peace of mind and a continual flow of clients. Once you stop resisting branding yourself, and concentrate on finding a target market and a profitable niche, you will become known as the expert in those circles.

What a day that will be for you, when it all becomes clear and makes it so much easier to attract the kind of clients you want; to understand their particular problems and in fact, help them reach their solutions faster and create the kind of vision you originally had for your business.

Trust me on this. I resisted branding for years. Like most service professionals, I fell into the trap of believing "Everyone needs my service."

But is 'everyone' your ideal client?

Here's a powerful strategy I request you use for attracting your ideal clients. I wholeheartedly recommend that you **Use the Universal Laws.**

In the early days of building my business, I sent out proposals to all types of clients. I thought whoever had a need and a checkbook, that was my client.

My focus changed by deciding what I didn't want in a client. I used that list and contrasted that with what I did want, and it has paid off tremendously. My stress level has become extinct and so will yours.

If you are struggling to attract your ideal clients, applying this concept will be like entering the twilight zone. Clients will come to you with less effort, and when they do come, they're exactly what you want to grow your business faster.

Having a strong team around you will maximize your strengths and exponentially increase your business. **Leading a Championship Support Team** is the perfect way to do this.

A good team should provide you with maximum support in all areas of your business and personal life. I know the first team member I got was a housekeeper to maintain order in my home, especially since I had a toddler in tow.

You don't have to hire an entire team at once or in fact pay them. If you're just starting out, you could use college students or family members. Then perhaps start to outsource your least profitable activities or your draining tasks as soon as you possibly can.

And after this is done, one of the only things you should focus on is creating and maintaining client satisfaction. How do you do that?

By **over delivering, over responding and WOWing your clients.** Hey, finding new business is one thing, but keeping it is another. Create your own personalized customer experience.

There are so many ways to value your customers and keep them with you. If your business is mainly online, don't forget about using offline, more traditional methods such as newsletters and gifts in the mail. Simple things like taking swift action if there is a complaint will ensure the client knows that they are important.

What's also vital to remember is that by setting up systems to respond quickly to your client's needs, keeps them interested in your offerings because they know you value them. This doesn't have to take up a lot of your time either.

A perfect way to do this is to **understand basic web strategies.** Nothing has had such a powerful impact in the 21st century as the internet and truth be told, any business owner not using this amazing tool is throwing away money every second.

The internet allows you to grow your business at 'warp' speed! Effective tools such as autoresponder's to manage your email lists and send out messages to your clients, will change the face of your business.

However, despite what you may have heard about the "If you build it they will come" strategy to using the net, you've got to also **spring into action and create S.M.A.R.T goals.**

Knowing what you want is one thing. Knowing how to get it is another, and goal-setting is a critical part of achieving our desires.

Remember your very exciting 3-year vision I told you about? Well, that's your starting point to creating your goals.

By breaking down your bold vision into short 1-year vision statements, then into quarterly goals, monthly management steps, weekly focus points and daily tasks, there absolutely no way that you cannot achieve your initial big, bold, and exciting vision! Doing this certainly doesn't mean that you won't get side-tracked though.

Let me tell you about a huge mistake I made within my first 3 years in business. One that set my business back almost a year and I'm hoping that what I say here won't fall on deaf ears.

Spend wisely. Invest in your business and yourself.

What was my grave mistake? I invested in people, products and services that did not move my business forward.

Yes, I know that you are an entrepreneur, possibly a coach and wanting to help people is an integral part of your makeup. I caution you, however, to use your profits for the growth of your business ONLY, for at least the first 3 years.

Successful people invest in themselves, and successful businesses are a result of owners investing in themselves first and their business second.

I encourage you to spend your money on your business and on your personal growth by attending seminars and taking courses that will help you grow. I personally love attending seminars anyway. The networking opportunities and potential joint venture possibilities are endless and these can take your business to heights you could never even imagine.

So, what's my definition of a successful business? It's having a fabulous business where you love what you do, you have fun at it, make money from it and building it becomes almost effortless.

Isn't it time you said "Yes, my business IS Fabulous?!"

Service professional strategist, trainer and author, Sandra Baptist aka The Vision Queen™, teaches aspiring service professionals and small business owners how to achieve their vision of creating a FABULOUS business with less effort, and make more profit in less time. Sandra can be contacted via email at: Sandra@MyFabulousBusiness.com. Visit www.MyFabulousBusiness.com to secure your free report and audio on the "7 Roadblocks That Prevent Service Professionals From Making Their First 1 Million Dollar$ Within 3 Years."

CHAPTER 33

Radiant Design®—
The Heart of a Conscious Business

Donna Bell

"One of the highest qualities of self-actualized people is their ability to see beauty everywhere, and to source life from the presence of beauty."
~ WAYNE DYER, AUTHOR/SPEAKER

At the heart of any business, there resonates a current level of consciousness. When you look at your office, do you feel inspired and full of life, or do you feel depressed and want to leave? As human beings we strive for consciousness. What we end up doing is organizing and moving stuff around, only to store our emotions in banker boxes and filing systems to be revisited another day.

However, it does not have to be that way. Until you have a profound relationship with your physical space, your business cannot reflect who you really are. An unconscious workplace is often cluttered and disorganized. Consequently this chaotic state influences an owner or employee to disengage from their work.

Engaged workers produce more, make more money for the company, and derive an emotional connection to each other. This atmosphere generates loyal customers, individuals tend to stay with the company longer, and are committed to greater quality and growth.

"Hanging on" to useless information costs a business time, productivity and profit. Frustration and fear may occur as they anxiously look for lost documents. Each piece of paper is valuable to them, when in fact it interferes with effectiveness, efficiency and the results that they plan to produce. Often, individuals will defend these monuments of clutter to the bitter end.

When coming from the place of Radiant Design®, you have the ability to create a profound space. Do not just take my word for it; this is your opportunity to prove it to yourself right now!

Take a moment and stand in your office, in front of your desk or anything that draws your attention. Have a pen and tablet in hand. Draw a line down the middle of the page. At the top of the left side write the words "physical" and on the right side, write "emotional."

Look closely at your office, desk or surroundings (I suggest that you apply this process to your employee's environment as well). Describe the physical condition. Are there things piled up, spilling over or in disarray? Do you have a stapler with out staples? Is the date on your calendar correct? When people enter your workspace, what do they most often notice? What is the overall setting and atmosphere like in your office? With "detail" examine the physical condition that is present in your office or desk area. Write this down, thank you.

Next, I want you to address the emotional feelings you have. Does it energize you? Do you feel drained? Is it an inviting experience? Write down all of the emotions that you have about your office, desk or anything that calls to you. Do you feel guilty? Are you frustrated? What is it like when you enter your room? Is your desk covered up? Are there things to repair?

The degree to which we are conscious within our physical environment is directly correlated to the degree in which we excel and receive what we desire for our business. Each object has an emotional attachment to it either positive or negative. When anything in your office is not uplifting, this tends to unwittingly drain your relationships, productivity and finances.

An item intentionally placed within your environment creates space, by inspiring you to see what is next. What does your office indicate regarding the success of your company? As previously stated, things piled up and spilling over, are a good indication of overwhelm and loss of attention to the details in your business.

Where in your business do you tend to procrastinate? Are your finances being put off? An empty stapler may seem to be of no consequence, but this is not true. A filled stapler is like a balanced checkbook --- everything in alignment. Look at what it might mean to have a calendar on your desk that is not showing the correct date. You might notice whether your business is operating up to date, yet with what extent of impeccability? Bravo! It takes great courage to look and listen from this level of detail.

Take to heart everything that you have written down and soulfully examine it. Each word is an indication of what is really going on. Your physical environment does not lie. When you write down frustration, overwhelm and fear, these words are not just descriptions of emotions. They also indicate that you have uncovered unconscious truths or conditions that have been continuously tolerated in your business. As you alter your consciousness by removing the clutter, it brings forth an everlasting change in your company that is immediately tantamount to fulfilling your dreams.

What astounds me is how hard people work to launch a new innovative business and end up with something ordinary. Passion is soon replaced by survival - merely "putting up with or getting by." The spark has gone out! We may start out highly attentive to detail, excited and motivated by order and flow, yet as time passes, our environment starts to exhibit neglect, becomes congested, and uninviting. We tend to put our business first and think that it is the highest priority. We ignore our built-up clutter as our work environment collapses. Unbeknownst to us this erodes the very foundation that we initially created, --- our "*Passion and Profit.*"

The following story is an example of this:

As I approached the company grounds, I was entranced by the regal architecture. It was breathtaking. Inside colors, shapes and textures flooded my senses as I saw the glorious furniture fabrics that complemented the draperies, tapestries and carpets. Everything was orchestrated to such a level of detail that I could see beauty in every corner. I was impressed! This was a company of great integrity. Could there really be any disorder?

As I arrived inside Rebecca's office, I spied unopened boxes in corners. A beautiful, carved, mahogany desk was barely appreciated, as it was covered with files, papers, and myriads of unfinished projects. Underneath it were more boxes and papers scattered on the floor. As a manager she was amazed that by simply looking at her office, I could determine the exact work related issues that she was facing.

At the onset, our team took everything out of her office piece by piece. We taught her our special process related to beauty and assisted her in experiencing an "I come first" attitude. From there, we evaluated every item as to its use or value in the business. As Rebecca got in touch with this, she was able to see excess and how she had never delegated or set boundaries.

Many of her projects were other people's workloads. This woman was buried in other people's expectations while resourcing unnecessary information. Taking on everyone else's tasks caused her to lose sight of having a nurturing environment. The more that was let go, the more she freed up. Within a few hours she had an office that was clear, filled with joy and productivity. It became apparent that she was not serving anyone by taking on their responsibilities. Her face was radiant (as well as her desk), and from this point on she would become a passionate and effective leader.

While the team and Rebecca were busy cleaning her office, the employees began to clear out their own workspaces. This bustling community awakened to a new found purpose in serving each other and the company. Who would have dreamed that the cleaning and clearing of her environment, would affect the entire department!

Upon entering her beautifully designed office, she was greeted by a dazzling display of Latin American dancers (brought from home). This uplifted and energized her, as she let the beauty of her workplace dictate what belonged and what did not.

People's judgments had affected her, even though she produced good results. These judgments fell away, as individuals stepped into her now radiant office. They were moved beyond what they had ever known possible for a work environment.

A few months later her division was awarded a stunning bronze plaque and a department bonus. This was given for the quality of their work, fulfillment of quotas and their ingenuity in designing innovative projects that forwarded the company's vision and profitability.

These are the results of Radiant Design®. Through the experience of beauty internalized from a Radiating Point®, ("personal values clarification process") unprecedented acceleration and abundance occur. It gives rise to "Radiant Life" as you embrace your business from a different realm; one in which your outer world aligns with your true self.

To excel rather than adapt ... to have extraordinary results ...to enter a new world that directs you as you surrender to your Radiating Point® ... that is the promise of this innovative proprietary training, coaching and consulting.

What would our world be like if it was filled with conscious businesses? Enter the world of Radiant Design® and see for yourself.

Donna Bell is a former radio talk show host and author of Radiant Design e-books series (insightful guides that uncover your attitudes and behaviors which perpetuate clutter and diminish your success). Personal Life Coach/ Consultant, of 15 years, designed Radiant Design®/Radiating Point® trainings and materials delivered to corporations, small businesses and communities. Celebrate by signing up for our free Radiant Design ezine and receive your e-book gift "Radiant Office Management"! Special Offer/Discounted Coaching available to readers at www.RadiantDesignBusiness.com.

CHAPTER 34

Unleash the Power of Giving in Your Business

Irene Dorang

If you're reading this book it's because you've been presented with a huge opportunity.

For whatever reason - whether it's because you live in a country that encourages free enterprise; because you were born with a high risk tolerance and a strong need for self-expression; because one morning at 3 a.m. that great idea popped into your head (yes, the one you scribbled notes about for two hours because you knew you could build a business on it) – for any or all of those reasons, you've been presented with the opportunity of entrepreneurship.

Now I'm not saying that opportunity by itself creates an easy road. Smart business ideas still take work to develop and sell, and plenty have failed because of mistakes made along the way.

(Show me a successful entrepreneur, and I'll show you someone who has learned some hard lessons on their path to the top!)

But the fact remains, if you're an entrepreneur or are considering becoming one, it's because *you've been given the opportunity* to do so.

And that's a gift.

So why do I bring this up?

Well, because understanding that and *acting* upon it are some of the most important things you can do with your business.

Understand what you've been given

It's very easy to get completely wrapped up in the process of developing a business, especially a new one. Product creation! Outsourcing! Tech problems! Customer service, continual learning, mastermind groups, teleseminars, copywriting…. Sound familiar?

But here's something we should always keep in mind.

While we're engrossed in our day to day endeavors, there are millions of people who, because of some random fact like the country they were born into, or the political circumstances they happen to live under, will never have the opportunity to do what we do.

Never. Even if, given the chance, they would come up with an idea ten times better than the one we're working on. Even if they would be the next Google or YouTube. They simply won't have the option.

Here's what's even more hard-hitting. For a lot of these people, the dream isn't entrepreneurship, it's getting through the day alive. You really don't have to look far to see what I mean. Just click onto a major news website and read nearly any story about Africa. I can almost guarantee you that within a week you'll see something that will have your hair standing straight up on end.

I don't say this to be depressing, but to make this point: If you live in a country where there's reasonable access to food, clean water, health care and education, and no one is going to shoot you or your relatives for voicing a political opinion, statistically you've already made the big-time. Millions would trade a limb just to be in your shoes.

If, in addition to that, you happen to have some good ideas and the chance to start your own business (and if you have Internet access, you can start any sort of virtual business), you've seriously hit the jackpot.

Even if you do nothing with your business idea or it ends up not working out, simply by having the *opportunity*, you're holding a winning lottery ticket.

Congratulations! But remember – most of these criteria had nothing to do with you. They were *gifts*.

Unleash the power of giving back

So, what concept does this naturally lead us to? Well, by now you probably have a pretty good idea that I'm going to say it's important to give back.

I realize that many entrepreneurs already do this. Even if you don't, it's likely in your plans for the future. This is great, because incorporating giving into your entrepreneurial philosophy unleashes a very powerful positive force into your business and your life.

I have experienced this personally, and it's a well-regarded concept. The words "whoever sows generously will also reap generously" date back to the Bible (2 Corinthians 9:6), and recently books and movies about what is commonly called The Law of Attraction have gained a lot of popularity.

So whether you believe as I do, that "From the one who has been entrusted with much, much more will be asked" (Luke 12:48), or you embrace a philosophy of spreading good karma, or you're simply motivated by a strong sense of fair play, it's likely that you understand the importance of giving back.

What's not so obvious is why many of us unintentionally fall short in that area. Let me explain.

The truth about what it takes

Who wants to leave the world a worse place than they found it? No one, right? But think about this:

If you asked a typical entrepreneur what his or her personal goals were in starting a business, one of the answers you'd hear would be "to provide a better life for myself and my loved ones."

That is a worthwhile goal. However, *everyone* has that goal. It comes naturally to us.

If they're not also working to provide a better life for someone they *don't* know – someone who wasn't gifted with all the advantages we talked about earlier – I believe they're going to end up leaving the world a little worse than they found it. (It reminds me of someone checking out of a hotel room leaving a bed full of mussed up sheets, and no tip for the housekeeper.)

There are so many forces driving the world in the wrong direction that *it takes extra effort on our part just to bring things back up to even.*

A good analogy is what happens with physical fitness. If I go through my normal daily life doing only what comes naturally to me – working at the computer, walking my dog, hiking occasionally and eating pretty reasonably – my fitness level doesn't stay the same. It decreases. (Trust me, I've tested this many times.)

In order to *maintain* my fitness level I actually have to put forth effort by doing more than just what comes naturally to me. Sometimes that involves choosing the less comfortable option.

If the goal is to *increase* my fitness level, that requires an even greater effort. And in order to succeed, I need to plan around the fact that it's human nature to fall somewhat short of our established goals.

If our primary goal is to help ourselves and our loved ones (and then, when we're ready, someone else), we may never get around to helping the "someone else." Or, when we do, it's likely to be later or less generously than we'd originally planned.

So how can we do better? First, by acknowledging that after having been given comparatively so much, it's only right that we step up to the plate and try. Then, by understanding how much effort it really takes, and planning around our shortcomings so that we succeed.

Think of it as operating on a universal honor system. Keep in your mind a realistic perspective of *everything* you've been given and give back accordingly.

Some thoughts on giving....

Concentrate on what you do, not on what others don't do

You can't save the world all on your own. However, ask yourself this question:

"If everybody else did what I'm doing, would the world be better or worse off?"

If the answer is "better", then keep doing it. (By the way, this is a good litmus test for life in general.)

Don't become overwhelmed by the scope of the problem

Even if you only help one person in this life whom you otherwise would not have touched, it makes a world of difference to that individual. Never underestimate how important that is.

A little can go a long way

One bright side to the enormous economic disparity in the world is that even small sums of money make a difference.

For example, twenty dollars often feeds ten people at your local homeless shelter. Thirty-one dollars through Mercy Corps pays for one month's worth of medicine and a doctor's salary in a third world country. One hundred twenty dollars to Girls Be Ambitious sponsors a year of school for a Cambodian girl who otherwise would have to work in the fields or the sex trade.

Color your perspective

If people in need were standing in front of us it would be a no-brainer – we'd be reaching into our pockets without even thinking. So, visit them occasionally. Spend some time each week checking human interest stories on websites like The New York Times and BBC News.

Use time wisely... while you have it

When it comes to giving, there's always a reason to put things off, but no one is guaranteed another day. So, ask yourself, "If tomorrow turns out to be my last day, is there someone on this earth besides the people I know whose life is better because I lived?"

The beautiful thing about giving back is that it's easy to turn that answer into "yes."

Make giving an integral part of your entrepreneurship, and watch your business resonate with greater energy, purpose and passion.

Irene Dorang is the founder and owner of The Agent Guide LLC. Her company provides easy-to-use, client-generating tools for real estate agents at www.ToolsForRealEstate.com. Contact Irene at Irene@ToolsForRealEstate.com or 1-877-449-0426. Get free real estate tips and see a list of Irene's favorite charities at www.ToolsForRealEstate.com/blog/.

CHAPTER 35

The "Three R's" for the 21st Century: How Readiness, Willingness to Risk, and Relationship Skills Provide a Sustainable Competitive Advantage

Cynthia Stamper Graff

Do you remember the "the three R's" from your elementary school days? Back when I was a kid, we were told that the three R's of a good education were "reading, 'riting, and 'rithmetic." While that might have been right for the 20th century, I use an updated set of "R's" to meet the challenges of today.

The First "R": Readiness

"One important key to success is self-confidence, and an important key to self-confidence is preparation."

~ ARTHUR ASHE

Luck, they say, is the intersection of preparation and opportunity. While opportunities often present themselves at the most unexpected moments and sometimes in the most unlikely ways, preparation is what allows us to recognize those moments, to assess which opportunities are golden, and to make something of them. Recognizing those moments and being prepared to make the most of them is the sign of a conscious entrepreneur.

I call it "readiness"—that state of mind in which "all systems are go." When you're operating in a state of readiness, you're interested and informed on the subject at hand. You're engaged and tuned in to what people are talking about, and in the process you're scanning the culture and the media for emerging trends and patterns. With technology and the world moving as quickly as it does, what qualified as "ready" even six months ago could be old news today.

Readiness is a never-ending process. It requires an innate curiosity about what's happening in the world, as well as a commitment to not just staying informed, but to being truly open to new information. For me, being ready includes regularly reading more than 40 different newspapers, magazines, professional journals and blogs each month—everything from the *New England Journal of Medicine* to the *National Enquirer*. I also make a point to talk with a wide variety of people—and to really listen to what they have to say. You'd be surprised at what you can learn by striking up a conversation at an airport bookstore or listening as people chat on a flight.

Readiness also means optimizing the state of our own minds. I'll always be grateful to my father for giving me Napoleon Hill's *Think and Grow Rich* when I was just 18 years old. In reading that book, I learned the value of setting a goal, writing it down, and then actively visualizing that it has already come to be.

This visualization process came in handy early in my career when I was a real estate developer in Salt Lake City. I once had to make payroll in less than a week and I didn't have enough cash in the bank to do it. I set my goal—to make payroll—and I started writing affirmations stated in the present tense: "I, Cynthia, enjoy having abundant cash…. I, Cynthia, enjoy having abundant cash." For days, I filled a yellow legal pad by writing that affirmation over and over. I also visualized myself at the bank with dollar bills sticking out of my pockets and overflowing out of my purse. I did this several times a day. The day before payroll was due, I received an unexpected refund check from the IRS. It was a check that enabled me not only to make payroll, but to replenish my savings!

Our thoughts are powerful, and I know from countless experiences like this one that we indeed tend to attract what we think about. While this concept was recently popularized by the bestseller, *The Secret*, the real secret is that it's always been true—and continues to be true. So, figure out what it is that you truly want and prepare your mind. **Get ready to receive it!**

The Second "R": Risk

"If you always do what you've always done, you'll always get what you always got."

~ ANN KAISER STEARNS, PH.D.

This quote from psychologist Ann Kaiser Stearns resonates so deeply for me that I featured it on the opening page of my first book, *Lean for Life*. For me, it's a gentle reminder that intentional change is an active, conscious choice. Change is the result of what we choose to do—or choose *not* to do—and inherent in that process is an element of risk.

In the summer of 1988, I was living in Toronto. I had been living there for eight years and absolutely loved it. My parents were visiting from Southern California, and we were enjoying a glass of wine in the garden one afternoon after playing golf. My father told me he was ready to retire and was seriously thinking about selling his company, Lindora, which he began in 1971 with a single weight loss clinic.

I told him, "Dad, the good news is you've built a great company, and you have a strong program and loyal patients. But there's so much left for you to do! The clinics look awful. Your staff needs nicer uniforms and a formal training program. You need a line of nutritional products. You also need to advertise. If you're going to sell the company, why not improve its value before you do?"

He looked at me, smiled and said, "I'm not going to do any of that. But you can come home and do it if you think you can. And if you do, maybe Lindora will be in the family for a long time." In a heartbeat, I was presented with a challenge—and a risk. Should I risk the great life and career I had created in Toronto to return home to Southern California and face the challenge of transforming my father's company? Was it a risk worth taking?

Twenty years later, I know the answer. It's an unqualified yes. The company's evolution and growth exceeded my wildest expectations. Today,

Lindora enjoys a reputation as America's leading medical weight control system. And most importantly, I'm the mother of an amazing 16-year-old daughter who I never dreamed 20 years ago would come into my life. So many of the blessings that today give my life such depth and meaning would have never occurred if I had played it safe and not welcomed the risk as an opportunity.

A few years ago, I read the results of a survey in which a group of octogenarians were asked what they would do differently if they could live their lives over. What do you think was the most common answer? I would have expected such responses as "I would work less and play more" or "I would spend more time with my family and friends" or "I would save more money." I was surprised by the number one answer: "I would have taken more risks."

When you're 80 years old, what will *you* wish you had done differently? **Are you more likely to regret the risks you've taken—or the ones you didn't take?**

The Third "R": Relationships

"Business is a cobweb of human relationships."

~ H. ROSS PEROT

Years ago, I attended a lecture that had a profound impact on me. The speaker addressed the escalating speed of change and explained how, at one point, it had taken more than two-thousand years for our recorded knowledge base to double. But in recent years, thanks to technological advances, our entire knowledge base is now doubling in less than two years! He explained how as soon as any product is launched, it can be reverse engineered and knocked off by competitors. A designer dress unveiled on a Paris runway can be photographed by cell phone and replicated in China within days. Weeks later, it can be on store shelves throughout the United States.

I was struck by what the speaker said next. He strongly argued that the one sustainable competitive advantage for the future will be the ability to quickly form and nurture intimate relationships. Business is conducted by people! To excel, it's critical to cultivate an ability to quickly assess a person's character, and then build a relationship that acknowledges mutual vulnerability.

In 2006, Lindora made a strategic decision to partner with Rite Aid Pharmacy and open the first in-store health care clinics in America to also offer medically-supervised weight control programs and services. At the time that we were finalizing the contracts, Rite Aid was in the middle of a major acquisition. As a result, the contracts were delayed. It was critical to both parties that our first clinic open on schedule. Any hope of meeting that deadline required that we move full throttle. We were down to the wire and either decision—to wait or to proceed—had significant potential risks and consequences.

Based on the strong relationship that I had established with Rite Aid senior management, I decided to assume the risk and spend the money to meet the pressing deadlines without having final, signed contracts in hand. It was a gut decision I made for one simple reason: I trusted the relationship. That decision turned out to be a good one. One year later, we had opened five Lindora Health Clinics and had more in the pipeline. Rite Aid also began selling our nutritional products in their more than 440 Southern California locations.

As a company, we prepared and we were **ready**. We were willing to take **risks,** and we put faith in our ability to build strong **relationships**. In business—as in life—those three "R's" can make all the difference.

Cynthia Stamper Graff is president and CEO of Lindora, Inc., America's leading medical weight control system. She is the author of three books, including the bestselling Lean for Life, and was the 2006 recipient of a National Association of Women Business Owner's "Remarkable Women" Lifetime Achievement Award. To learn more about Lindora, visit www.lindora.com.

CHAPTER 36

6 Essential Insights of a Conscious Leader

Stephanie Graziano

I've had the Entrepreneurial bug for as long as I can remember. As a child I was the one who always wanted to play business, who wanted to have the lemonade stand, and who would designate others to roles of managers or sales persons so that I could go off and create our next business. I would often wonder though, why would the other kids so readily follow me and fall into the places I designed for each of them? Why didn't I ever run into the kid who would ask, "Who left and put you in charge?" What was the key to making everyone feel a necessary part of the whole success? These and many other leadership keys would become a focus of my quest to understand successful entrepreneurship.

Since those early childhood days, I've spent more than 30 years making my way up the ladder in the Entertainment industry, and owning my own companies, sometimes leading teams of several hundreds of people, in multiple countries, on a dozen different projects. The cultures may be different, but the foundations of great entrepreneurial leaders remain the same. I've spent a lot of time focusing on the traits of great Conscious Leaders and have used what I learned to turn several new businesses into fun places for people to work. I am now proud to coach Women Entrepreneur's in search of insights to becoming Conscious Leaders themselves.

One of the most common challenges among the entrepreneur's I work with is the perception that managing is leading. Nothing could be further from reality. Most women are natural managers, able to multi-task and determine how each member of a team can contribute. They are good diplomats and can soothe hurt feelings. But being a conscious leader, a person others will not only follow, but also be inspired to create for and support fully, takes a real conscious mind of a leader. Here are my **"Essential Six"** tips for becoming a successful entrepreneur and Conscious Leader.

Honesty – Acknowledging your strengths and weaknesses and those of your team, is crucial to being a conscious leader. Being really clear with your team about what you expect of them and of yourself will help everyone understand their measure of success. If people are unclear of your expectations, you leave them open to failure, and thus you will fail as a leader.

When our focus is on leading others, we sometimes spend a lot of time trying to be someone we would look up to, rather than who we are. Great conscious leaders are able to share their strengths with others and admit their weak areas. They are also able to assist members of their team in doing the same without any judgment.

This is really important. When team members feel comfortable with exposing their true selves and confident that you are there to help them rise to their higher abilities, they will be anxious to follow your lead. They will understand that your success and their success are tied together and heartfelt. People follow conscious leaders who they feel will be honest with them and work with them to reach success without judging the starting place, and who celebrate everyone's accomplishments.

Objectivity – Not bringing your own baggage to the party is a hard thing to do. We have lived so many years, and have so many different life experiences. These are the things that help to shape us, right? Yes... and no. Our experiences do help to shape us, but we have the ability to take away from each experience what we feel will benefit us the most. Embrace every new opportunity and experience with a fresh and open heart. Try not to burden a new experience with the disappointments from another.

When you are trapped by past disappointments and failures, you are more apt to cause the very problems you are trying to avoid. Remember that each and every person on your team also have had many years of experience. Having an open mind and heart will allow you to benefit from someone else's positive experience. Sometimes it's the fresh perspective that will bring about the perfect solution. When you are unable to be objective, you may miss the exact opportunity you were looking for.

So be conscious, take a chance, and understand that not every situation will turn out the same as the last. Many elements may be different and the same approach may well yield a new outcome.

Respect – If you don't respect yourself first, you can't have respect for others. You got here for a reason. Be proud of what you've accomplished, yet don't be boastful. Just know that you are worthy of the position you have made for yourself. Others will sense your self respect, and when you lead by example and are respectful of others, they will return the favor.

I have seen many reluctant leaders struggle with their team. They fear giving up any compliments or secrets that may have allowed them to move up into a leadership position. I say forget about them. Let yourself be the example. You became a leader because you have strengths that others are looking for. Embrace the idea that you can share your knowledge without losing any ground, and show others the same respect. Compliment their good ideas and work well done. Give credit where it is due.

Building respect as a conscious leader will come from having respect for yourself and others, and by showing it. Being sure of your accomplishments, being respectful and not boastful, and leading by example will prove to gain you many followers.

Intuition – What does your little inner voice say? Do you take the time to listen? Do you understand how instrumental it has been in getting you to where you are today? When something is bothering you, there's usually a good reason. Listen to that - let it guide you to **conscious questions**. Be sensitive to your instincts as there is a big difference between taking a risk and not listening to your gut.

Conscious leaders are in tune with their little inner voice. They take a breath and ask, "What is this that seems to be nagging at me?" Ask yourself creative questions, conscious questions, in an effort to get to the bottom of the situation. Don't become frightened or self judging, as that will only keep you from the truth. Once you have uncovered the concern, you might find that it provided a chance to re-evaluate and included a very important step or person you had overlooked.

Intuition is a strength. It takes time to develop and can become one of your best allies. Listen to it when it speaks to you, as there is a reason behind its voice - big or small, good or bad - and it will help you in your efforts to remain a true conscious leader.

Connection – John Maxwell says, "Leaders touch a heart before they ask for a hand." Make **conscious** connections and build relationships. When you take the time to get to know your team, client, or partner - what they value, what motivates them - and you can celebrate the small successes, you will find it worth millions. People are dedicated to leaders who care about them - leaders who take the time to understand what they need and to make themselves clear. Don't underestimate the power of forming strong personal relationships.

When I am dealing with my team, I realize that not everyone is the same. Some have outgoing personalities while others are quiet and like to work alone. I like to understand each of their particular needs, desires, and styles, so that we can create an environment that works best for all of us. Having a personal connection means the other person feels you care. It doesn't mean getting involved in gossip circles, personal dramas, or displacing your values or the values of your business. It simply means being conscious of those around you in a way that allows you to give and get the very best from them in return.

Empowerment – You can't do it by yourself. The first thing a great leader learns is that you need a team. Teach them well and give them room to grow.

Many leaders forget what it was like coming up the ladder. Some leaders find themselves in leadership positions and don't even know how they got there.

Be very clear with yourself. Building a powerful team is essential to being a successful conscious leader. Empowering your team is critical. Your team is a reflection of your skills. Teaching is about allowing others to achieve the results by doing.

Empowerment is a crucial part of being a leader. Teach well and empower others to carry out the tasks at hand. Compliment and reward their success and you have done your job well. Being a conscious leader means understanding the difference between getting the job done and doing it yourself. When your team is empowered, you will have more time to grow a conscious business.

Stephanie Graziano, Founder and Success Coach, BYOB; Building Your Own Business, believes in the Conscious team leader. Her coaching focus is on Women Entrepreneurs looking to increase their confidence, credibility, and visibility. She has been interviewed by CNN, The Los Angeles Business Journal, the Los Angeles Times, and Business Start-Ups Magazine. Please visit our website - www.buildingyourownbusiness.com, or contact us at (818) 515-0006.

CHAPTER 37

Writing: A Journey of Creativity, Consciousness, and Connection

Julie Isaac

Writing is one of the most powerful vehicles there is for sharing the fullness of your soul and your business with others. Whether you're writing a blog post, an article, or a book, it allows you to communicate—heart to heart—your core beliefs and values, your passion, the knowledge and wisdom you've gained through experience, and all you have to offer. But before your writing can reach out into the world and touch even one other heart; before it can begin building relationships, establishing you as an expert, and bringing you business; the writing process, itself, will dive deep into your own heart and take you on a journey of creativity, consciousness, and connection.

Igniting Creativity

Writing arises from, as well as ignites, your creativity. An eternal circle, writing is a subtle dance between inspiration and craft, between consciously creating and letting go into the creative flow. These two energetic movements are the in and out breaths of creativity, each bringing their own precious gifts to whatever you're writing.

Inspiration and writing in flow are where spirituality and creativity meet. They are the outward expression of your inner connection with source, of your being fully present and at one with the task at hand—writing. Because of this relationship between spirituality and creativity, lighting candles, meditation, prayer, or any other practice that invokes the sacred, or connects you with your higher power, will help open your mind and heart to the words and ideas that will best serve you, your business, and those you want to reach with your writing.

To open even more deeply to inspiration and writing in flow, you need to make peace with the unknown. Even when you're working from an outline, or know your material well, writing wants to lead you into uncharted territory—to what's new, to what's unique, to what's you. To what's arising in this moment. If you can see the unknown as mysterious and delightful, rather than uncomfortable or stressful, it will be easier to relax into your writing and let it surprise you.

- How do you connect with your creative source?
- What can you do to expand and deepen your connection?

Expanding Consciousness

Even when your writing flows, it will challenge and change you. Its essence is transformation. Whether you're exploring new ideas or material you've worked with for years, writing will compel you to question your assumptions, look at the familiar in new ways, and seek clarity and wisdom. It will call you to connect with your deepest knowing, and to express yourself from there with purpose, integrity, and compassion. Writing is more than an avenue of self-expression; it's a vehicle for self-discovery.

If you have any doubts, fears, or issues around writing, self-expression or success, expect them to surface. When they do, welcome and work with them. This is your opportunity for healing—to see through, and let go of, what gets in your way.

- What gets in the way of your moving forward with clarity and confidence?
- Are you willing to tell the truth about, and let go of, what gets in your way?

Making Connections

We write to be read. When someone reads your blog post, article, or book, you're talking to them. They're hearing your words, thinking about your ideas, and feeling like they're getting to know you.

This sense of connection can deepen your relationship with existing clients and customers, or attract new ones. It can encourage feedback, increase your credibility, and grow your business. Whether you're taking your readers step-by-step through a single process, or showing them the big picture, it's an intimate conversation—even if you never get to see, meet, or know them. And with the Internet, this conversation has gone global.

- What message, or vision, do you want to share through your writing?
- How do you want your words to affect, or change, your readers?

Writing With Ease

If you enjoy writing, fabulous! Take paper and pen, or get on your computer, and fly. You can brainstorm and then organize your ideas, or simply let loose and see where your writing takes you. However, if the idea of writing makes you a little nervous, you can talk your way through your first draft. You can dictate your ideas into a tape recorder, be interviewed by a friend or colleague, or record a live presentation. These recordings can be transcribed into a written draft of your article or book, which you will then review and revise.

The beauty of creating content in a variety of ways, such as brainstorming, writing, being interviewed, and giving a live presentation, is that each of these creative mediums inspires a slightly different response. Although the basic information you want to cover usually remains the same, someone interviewing you will elicit a slightly different set of feelings, ideas, memories, and stories, than you would come up with sitting alone in a room, writing. Mixing your mediums can actually fire up your creativity, and give your writing more dimension and depth.

If you find yourself procrastinating, writing in circles, or getting frustrated by the creative process, gently pull your focus away from your own experience and emotions. Then focus on a sense of service, instead. Whether you feel that you're serving your higher power, your idea, your project, your customers, or your business, seeing your writing as service can give you a higher sense of purpose, and help you solve and dissolve any challenges more quickly and easily.

It also helps your writing flow more smoothly when, as you're writing, you remember these three important principles:

- **Be yourself**

What makes your writing unique is you. Your heart. Your wisdom. Your experience. Your voice. Whether you're writing a memoir, a manifesto, or a training manual, the more your personality and passion appears on the page, the more you'll engage your readers and create a lasting relationship with them.

- **Inspiration is always available**

You've probably heard the phrase "What you focus on expands." It's true of writing, as well. If you're stuck, confused, or drawing a blank, remember: Where you focus, inspiration will flow.

There are two ways to focus your attention that will ignite inspiration. Like running with a kite to catch the wind, if you start researching, brainstorming, or writing, it will open up your creativity, and the aspects of your project that aren't clear, yet, will start to take shape. Or you can simply decide what you need in order to take the next step on your writing journey—whether it's information, direction, confidence, clarity, an idea, outline, or the right words—then get quiet, focus on it, and expect it to come. It will.

Even though I've experienced this a thousand times, it always feels like a miracle when the words, ideas, or direction I've been struggling for suddenly pops to mind because I stopped, took a deep breath, relaxed, and focused.

- **Any sense of struggle is an invitation to greater self-awareness and creativity**

If you're struggling with your writing in any way, instead of getting frustrated, get curious. What is the struggle trying to tell you? If you're procrastinating, is it because you don't know what comes next, or you've strayed from your vision, or you feel overwhelmed by what's going on in your life? Once you discover the cause of your struggle, the solution becomes clear—you need to brainstorm, or refocus, or do a little time management magic.

The important thing is to see any sense of struggle—whatever gets in the way of your writing with ease—as an invitation to go within and discover what you need to continue moving forward.

Julie Isaac, "the Brainstorming Queen," is a writer and creativity coach who helps authors and entrepreneurs get started, stay focused, and complete their writing projects, from blog posts to books. Julie's unique and innovative creativity tools—A Writer's Arithmetic™, The Book Writing Compass™, and more—make the journey from idea to manuscript easier and more fun. Email her at Julie@WritingSpirit.com, and download her free reports, "Blasting Through Writer's Block" and "Writing a One Page Book Proposal," at www.WritingSpirit.com.

CHAPTER 38

The 4 Components of Conscious Entrepreneurship

Christine Kloser

Conscious entrepreneurship. It's a phrase you resonate with and a concept you believe in. It's the term that captures the essence of who you are, what you stand for and how you conduct business. But, what exactly does it mean to be a conscious entrepreneur? How can you define this term in a way that makes it tangible and measurable… while remaining open to the infinite possibilities and gifts from the Universe? I'm glad you asked!

I'd like to share with you the four components of conscious entrepreneurship. This isn't anything I learned when I earned my Bachelor's degree in Business Management, and it's certainly nothing I learned on a tele-seminar or by reading popular business books. I've come to this definition through my personal experience and feeling drawn to integrate my spiritual nature into my business.

Component #1: A Conscious Business Makes Money

This was a very difficult concept for me to embrace. Like many conscious entrepreneurs, I cared a lot about my customers and clients; sometimes more than I cared about myself. I had been willing to sacrifice my own needs to help others, and I'd give away my time, my knowledge, my ideas, everything… without asking for anything in return. I wanted to be of service, and to help as many people as possible. So I did it at all cost—and it did cost me a bundle— because I didn't want to let anyone down. For that wouldn't be a conscious business, would it? Ha!

Sometimes it's challenging to combine your desire to "serve" with the desire to make money. Is it really possible to combine Mother Teresa and Donald Trump? Yes. I know these two energies feel like they go together as well as oil and water, but in order to be a successful and profitable conscious business owner you need both. Money is simply a form of energy that is exchanged for the service you provide to the world. You deserve to be well compensated for that!

I believe that in order for our world to survive (and thrive) through these rapidly changing times, it needs for you, the conscious entrepreneur, to make a lot of money, so you can spread more of your wisdom, love, knowledge, heart and soul out into the world... giving back in a BIG way!

If you looked up the definition of "business" in Webster's dictionary, you'd see something that says business is "a profit-seeking endeavor." If you do not seek, and realize, a profit, it is not a business. It is a charity; it is a sinking ship; it's something you'll begin to resent and dread because the lack of money drains every ounce of energy from your being. It's a great challenge to elevate to the higher energetic vibrations of Source energy when you don't have enough money for rent.

While we're on the topic of money, let's quickly clear something up here. You are meant to attract a lot of it. Not for the purpose of acquiring material possessions and being able to keep up with the Jones'. Instead, you're meant to receive a lot of money so you can keep up with your soul's desire to be fully-expressed in the world. Trust me, that plan is not for you to be in survival mode for the rest of your life.

Component #2: A Conscious Business Makes A Difference

The second component of a conscious business is to make a positive difference in the lives of others. A company that produces and markets a diet pill that is known to cause damage to the human body is not a conscious business.

Yet the consultant, whose deepest commitment is to transform their clients' lives, and quite possibly the world, by sharing their knowledge and wisdom, is a conscious business owner. Thankfully, there are many thousands of businesses that already operate under this context of conscious business. I'm sure you have experienced a few yourself aside from your own business.

For instance, if you have a carpet cleaning business it might not seem like it's making as much of a difference as an alternative medical practitioner who restores her patients back to health. But here's the truth. Carpet cleaning does make a difference in the lives of the people who are having their carpets cleaned. It's helping them live the kind of lifestyle they want to live. It's keeping a cleaner environment for their family. It's keeping a home where the homeowners are eager to open up their doors and invite in neighbors, friends and loved ones, to enjoy space and time in their home.

So a carpet cleaner, when you look at it close enough, truly is making a difference to their customers and clients. This should be the thing you keep in mind the most when you're working with a new customer or talking to one of your clients. It's truly connecting with the concept of how you can be of service to them, and how you can positively impact their lives. When you're operating as a conscious business owner, it's not just about closing a deal; it's about being of service and making a difference.

Occasionally this will mean you'll refer your prospect or client to somebody else, if that referral can better match the needs of your client. Because when you truly want to make a difference by serving your prospect or client as best as you possibly can, it might not always mean you are the best one to help them. This can be a very difficult concept to swallow, but it's an important one to embrace on your path of conscious business. And the beauty of this is that as soon as you release a prospect, you become a magnet for more of the right prospects to come to you.

This can be a very scary place to enter, especially when you feel like you "need the money." It is much easier to do when you believe 110% in yourself and your product or service, and you don't have any doubt about what you can (and cannot) provide your clients. The increased confidence you get from believing in yourself and your business is a necessary piece of being willing to go to these places to make a difference.

The other aspect to consider is not only in making a difference for each individual customer or client, but also connecting with the difference that you want to make in the world. How will your business positively transform others? What is the legacy you want to leave? How will your conscious business make the world a better place? How will you best serve the evolution of our society? These are valuable questions to ask yourself in relation to the second component of conscious entrepreneurship... making a difference.

Component #3: A Conscious Business Calls You To Be Fully Who You Are

If you've ever felt like you had to hide a piece of yourself in your business, it's not a conscious business. Rather, a conscious business draws forth every ounce of your spirit and calls you to be more of who you are. Your conscious business needs you to be who you are because that is exactly where your success lies.

Too often business owners feel like they "should" be a certain way in business, and a different way in life. It's just not true. The only way to succeed as a conscious business owner is to be ALL of you, ALL of the time. The very qualities and characteristics that make you, you, are the exact qualities and characteristics your business (and customers and clients) need you to be.

It's incredibly challenging to put on your "game face" while trying to fit into someone else's idea of who you should be. Or worse yet, your own misguided idea of who YOU think you should be. The joy truly comes in surrendering to exactly who you are.... yes, every tender loving ounce of your being; quirks, idiosyncrasies and all. Those are the things that make you who you are, who God meant for you to be from the moment you were born.

One side benefit of being fully who you are in your conscious business is that you have no "competition." Nobody can be you. Nobody can duplicate your heart and soul. Nobody can exude you, but you. So as you discover and express more of your essence, the more you distinguish yourself in an overcrowded market of entrepreneurs who are trying to be someone else. In so doing, you will only attract those customers and clients who are meant to work with you. You become a natural magnet for your best clients.

As we discussed in the second component, sometimes you may be the one to refer your client to someone else if they can be better served elsewhere. But how do you know if they're not the right fit for you? The answer is simple. If you feel yourself being compromised by actively pursuing the business, or you feel your dream becoming further out of reach, it's not the right fit. You'll know when this is happening because you won't feel called to be more of who you are; you may even feel like you're making yourself be less just to get the business. Watch out for this pitfall as it can ruin you and your business.

Being who you are is the strongest asset you can have as a business owner. The "secret formula" of you can never be cloned. And oh what fun it is to discover that your most important role in your business is to be more of your Divine self. How lucky you are that this is your highest mission in your business, and your life. How blessed you are that deep down inside, you probably already know this. Perhaps right now you're even nodding your head "yes" in thankful agreement that you get to discover and share more of yourself through your business. Awesome, isn't it!

Component #4: A Conscious Business Trusts In Its Divine Plan

The fourth component of conscious business success is to trust in your Divine Plan. This means to always know, no matter how challenging, no matter how much a particular client might be driving you up the wall, no matter how much you're pulled off track, that you continue to step forward in every moment and trust that your divine plan is perfectly unfolding in your life. And you do this without panicking when negative emotions start creeping in.

One of my clients asked, "What do I do when I feel lack or doubt coming into my mind and my divine plan is nowhere to be seen?" The answer is simple, but not necessarily easy in the moments of distress, and that is to reconnect back to Source energy. When you feel negative emotions rising within you, it's time to make a conscious shift away from the dark, downward spiral of the those emotions. You do this by elevating your awareness to the vibration of God/Source. By doing this it makes it easier to realize that the experience you're having is literally a "blip" in relation to the Divine Plan for your life. It is this elevation of consciousness that allows you to see the Divine Plan, so you can surrender to it and know that "all is well."

There are a myriad of ways to reconnect with Source and rediscover trust in your Divine Plan, but one of my favorite methods to shift my vibration and embrace trust in my Divine Plan is to listen to guided meditations. This is a tool I have and continue to use in my life, and I'm convinced that guided meditations were my saving grace when I experienced some huge challenges in my prior business. So I've made it easy for you to take advantage of this same tool. I've recorded a meditation for you to download immediately at www.LoveYourLife.com/meditation. It's called, "Trust in Your Divine Plan", and it'll gently guide you back to your trusting heart and peace of mind.

Have fun embracing these four components into your business. Let them guide you in making decisions, taking risks and following your heart as you build your business to make money, make a difference, call forth more of who you are... and fully express your Divine plan.

Christine Kloser is an inspirational business coach, engaging speaker, award-winning book publisher and author of The Freedom Formula: How to Put Soul in Your Business and Money in Your Bank. Since 1991 she has been an entrepreneur; continually exploring new ways to integrate her spiritual understandings with strategic business tactics for herself and her clients. She provides lectures, training, coaching and book publishing services to thousands of entrepreneurs worldwide. Get your FREE copy of Christine's Conscious Business Success Kit by visiting www.LoveYourLife.com today.

CHAPTER 39

Unleash Your Marketing Karma™

Kelly L. LeFevre, MSM and Molly Luffy, MBA

Imagine your most abundant business…growing, lively, and thriving. Making your dreams a reality, calling the shots, enjoying your vocation, taking more vacations!

Sounds pretty good, right? Isn't this what you dreamed of when you started your business? Of course it is! We all did at the start.

But if you're like the vast majority of business owners in the world, you were struck by a pretty intimidating reality shortly after you started your venture. You were going to have to market your company. Marketing? Who said anything about marketing?

You were dreaming of the freedom and the flexibility - being the captain of your own ship when you started your business, right? Not becoming a marketing expert. But there it was staring you right in the face. And you knew you *had* to figure out how to effectively market your business in order to be successful.

The key is finding a way to market your business that not only feels good to you, but creates a steady flow of prospects. Plus when you finally find a marketing strategy that feels natural and good, **and** it produces prospects, then, my friend you have struck marketing gold!

So if you agree the best marketing of all is that which you enjoy, feel confident about and works, then do we have a strategy for you! It's called Marketing Karma™ and it will revolutionize the way you think, feel and experience marketing your business.

What is Marketing Karma™?

The philosophy of Karma is simple - what you put out into the world is returned to you. "What goes around, comes around." Sound familiar?

Have you ever considered how Karma applies to business? Does the predatory lender have some bad mojo coming their way? Or does the small business owner who mentors an aspiring entrepreneur have good fortune ahead? We would say "Yes!" on both counts.

You can apply this universal law of cause and effect to successfully market your business. And when you unleash the power of your Marketing Karma™, you can easily grow your business simply by giving it away.

Yes, we said grow your business by giving it away...and just so we're clear, we do mean for free!

Here's how it works: when you do good things in the world as you market your business, they will be returned to you in more ways than you can conceive. By marketing your business in this way – a way that not only *does* good, but *feels* good to you - you'll have much more fun, be more at ease, and experience more success in your business.

Marketing Karma™ focuses on developing relationships with prospective clients versus the old, transactional-based way of marketing which encourages encountering someone, telling them what you do and asking for the sale right away.

These days people are much more business-savvy. They've been subjected to all of those "old school", hard-core sales and marketing techniques and frankly, they're turned off by them. No one wants to feel like they are being manipulated or sold to. Today people want to know, like and trust the people they do business with. Implementing the following innovative strategies will help you develop powerful, long-term relationships with people who may buy from you or may evangelize for your business – or both!

5 Strategies to Unleash Your Marketing Karma™

Here are five strategies to help you unleash your Marketing Karma™:

1. **The Pink Shovel™** – One of the best strategies to employ is offering a powerful, valuable version of your service, for free in the form of a sample. Think of Baskin Robbins™ "pink spoon" sample of ice cream. It's a taste, it's free, and it helps people experience what they are considering purchasing. The Pink Shovel™ is more than a one-time, small, free sample. It is a longer-term strategy designed to create practical, results-oriented, fabulous experiences that really deliver great value to your prospective clients, for free. This helps people begin to know, like and trust you before you ask them to purchase from you.

2. **Volunteering** – Donating your time and expertise to an organization is not traditionally thought of in terms of marketing, but it should be! Where else can you personally support an organization plus build quality relationships with people who may need your services or can refer other potential clients to you? Doing this helps get your name out there as someone who cares about a cause – and is willing to work to help that cause. What a great reputation builder!

3. **Sponsorships** – This strategy is perfect for the small business owner who wants to support an organization, but doesn't have much extra time to get involved. Think about your target market. Is there a trade or professional association conference you can sponsor? What about establishing a scholarship at a community college? Could you collaborate with several complimentary businesses to establish a foundation that serves your market in some way? The possibilities are endless!

4. **Mentoring** – Did anyone take you under their wing and show you the ropes at some point in your career? Maybe it's time you did the same thing. As a mentor, you can offer specific business advice, act as a sounding board, or teach your mentee your secrets to success. This relationship allows you to have a very positive impact on someone else's life.

5. **Apprenticeships** – During your career has someone offered you an opportunity to learn some real-life business skills? If so, wasn't it incredibly

beneficial to your professional development? Apprenticeships are truly a win-win proposition. You win by gaining extra time and help, and your apprentice wins by gaining valuable real-life business experience.

Give it away? Are you crazy?

Usually when we introduce the concept of Marketing Karma™, our audience has at least one of the following reactions:

"But people don't value free stuff." That's ridiculous! When you go to the grocery store and they are passing out free samples, do you try them? Or do you say, "I'm not going to taste it because it's free. Only food I pay for tastes good." Our guess is that you'll try the free samples and you may even buy the product if you like the taste.

"Why would I want to give away my services for free?" you might ask. It can be a challenge to shift from scarcity to abundance, especially if you've been taught to think business is a 'dog-eat-dog' world. Yet wouldn't it be nice to focus on building relationships and providing value instead of just "making the sale?" Marketing your business from a foundation built on abundance will help you focus on prosperity and you'll be amazed at what the Universe brings back to you!

"How am I going to make any money?" Make no mistake; Marketing Karma™ is not a 'get-rich-quick' scheme. It's a way of developing relationships with your potential customers right from the beginning. Over time you will offer them opportunities to buy from you once they've begun to know, like and trust you.

Tips for Success

Marketing Karma™ is "marketing you can feel good about." The key to successfully developing any of these strategies is shifting your mindset from the traditional, transaction-based marketing philosophy to long-term, relationship-based marketing. Here are some critical success factors to create an abundant business that not only thrives, but provides value in the world.

- Live life with an abundant mindset – "Of course I can give lots of my product away. I have so much to give!"

- Give as much as you can and then some more – for Marketing Karma™ to be really effective, your samples must be big and juicy and really valuable!
- Explain to people why you give it away – be open about your belief in Karma, and Marketing Karma™.
- Be unattached to the outcome – do it joyfully knowing it is a good thing to do. Remember, this is a longer-term strategy that takes time to work. Give it time, and trust in the positive benefits you'll experience.
- Be yourself – create a strategy that showcases your expertise and personality.

Why is It So Powerful?

Marketing Karma™ is a perfect marketing strategy to counteract today's world of information overload. Think about how many times a day you are bombarded with information, advertisements, calls to action, and people asking for your business.

This strategy positions your business as a quiet calm cutting through all this noise. Imagine yourself standing quietly with your hands stretched out in front of you, cradling a beautiful, valuable, high quality sample of your product or service. That's Marketing Karma™. Give it away. Provide value that enhances others' lives, and your kindness will be repaid to you in a positive way.

Who knows what positive outcomes await you? Perhaps one of these prospects will buy something from you. Perhaps they will tell others about you. Perhaps the local newspaper will hear of your generosity and do a big front-page feature on your unusually wonderful business platform...and for free!

So enjoy your business. Have more fun! And give it away. The possibilities the Universe has for you are endless!

Kelly L. LeFevre, MSM and Molly A. Luffy, MBA, authors of the upcoming book Unleash Your Marketing Karma: How to Build Your Business by Giving It Away™, are Co-Founders of the Business Building Roundtable. This free virtual community helps service-based solo & micropreneurs learn innovative strategies to grow and enjoy their businesses, so they may achieve their ultimate success and satisfaction. To get your free membership and special bonuses, visit http://www.BusinessBuildingRoundtable.com.

CHAPTER 40

Where is the Hidden Wealth in Your Business?

George Meidhof

If you're a conscious entrepreneur, you need to be aware of every aspect of your business if you really want to create wealth, and that includes the systems that make your business run. Even the most successful small business owners don't take out time to understand the true wealth in their business. They get up in the morning, ready to wage daily war on the business battlefront. They charge the ramparts; they conquer the enemy and feel good about what they accomplished. But they never take a moment to document the history they created! Anyone who has taken an American History class knows who Pickett was, and the details of his charge at Gettysburg. As you may recall they were out of ammunition and desperate to win the battle, so hand to hand combat became the order of the day. There are many history buffs in this country that can reenact that scene because it was well documented. Can you do the same for your business?

Your business challenges may not be as serious as Pickett's, but as a business owner, you solved it. Can you and your employees reenact that situation the next time the problem comes up? The key to mining the hidden wealth in your business is the systems that can be duplicated on demand and produce the same predictable results. Most franchises exist on the premise that they have a system that can be duplicated by others to achieve the same kind of results as the founders. The most common example is McDonalds®. They have a manual to cover all aspects of their business model. They tell you how to hire; how to handle the cash; how to thaw and cook the meat; how clean the bathrooms need to be etc. Everything is explained in detail. As a consumer, we walk into any McDonald's and know the experience will be the same as the last McDonald's we visited. Can your customers say the same thing about your business? Is the experience always predictable from your customer's point of view? Better yet, is it always a positive experience as well?

Documenting your company policies, processes, procedures and systems provides the conscious entrepreneur with three major benefits. First, the value of your business to a potential purchaser is greatly enhanced. McDonald's gets $1,000,000 for their franchise rights because it is 100% duplicatable. The easier it is for a potential buyer to step in and take over the reins immediately when they buy the business, the higher the price you business will command when the time comes for you to sell.

The second major benefit is to prevent a single employee from holding you hostage. How many times have you seen a business deteriorate when a key employee leaves? Questions come up and people say "Sally used to handle that", but no one knows exactly how Sally did handle it. Simple process documents would allow another person to step in and handle the situation with ease. Being able to prove that a single employee can't hold the business hostage will enhance the salability of your company.

The third major benefit to the conscious entrepreneur is personal freedom. You no longer have to do everything yourself. You can leave behind that stage of business growth where "you" are the business and become the blossoming enterprise you envisioned when you started. When all the policies, procedures and systems are documented, you can feel confident that the business will hum along smoothly during your absence.

All of this sounds fine, but I always get two major objections from my clients. They reply "Nobody can do it like me", and "Isn't that an awful lot of work to write everything down?"

On the first issue, you are absolutely right when you say that no one can do it like you! And that's because we are all different people. The key is to focus on results. Can someone else produce the same results as you, doing it their way? Let me give you an example. Last night a friend of mine was telling me about a problem that occurred in his business while he was out of state running a program for a client. One of the critical collateral items was sent to his office rather than to the meeting site. His employees back at the office alerted him of the problem and he spent the entire day developing a resolution. It seems FedEx will divert a package to a new location for their account holders for a fee. Unfortunately he did not have an account with FedEx and spent hours searching for someone with an account to help him out. He finally resolved the problem when he found a business associate with a FedEx account that was willing to assist with the shipment, by allowing him to use the associate's FedEx account. Now the question my friend should be asking from this experience is does he have a written process in place for his employees to follow the next time this situation arises? If not, he had better be prepared to spend another 6 hours of his time the next time a delivery is sent to the wrong address.

Can someone execute this kind of plan with a simple set of instructions, and do it as well as the business owner? Certainly. Is this the best use of the business owner's time? No. How hard would it be to document this process? Easy. It might be something like: "Call in order, Joe Blow, John Doe, Jimmy Smith, until one of them answers and ask to use their FedEx account to divert a shipment. Agree on fee for the use of the account, and then refer to FedEx guidelines for special services to redirect the shipment." While this may be oversimplified, the process is not that difficult.

You can also ask your employees to document what they do. The steps for systemizing your business are actually quite easy. Start by creating an Operations Manual Binder including the following:

- Organization Chart and Position Descriptions
- Identify specific tasks to be systemized
- Pick one task
- Owner: Identify ideal procedure and expected result
- Flowchart ACTUAL procedure

- Compare to ideal
- Brainstorm for best and most SIMPLE procedure
- Flowchart NEW procedure
- Write text of new procedure, Include "why"
- Test procedure using unrelated person
- Adjust flowchart
- Rewrite text
- Put in Operations Manual Binder
- Repeat

The areas of the business that really should be systemized are:

- Marketing
- Sales
- Human Resources
- Customer Service
- Purchasing
- Inventory control
- Manufacturing
- Accounting
- Operations
- Technology
- Other office processes, such as telephone protocol, greeting visitors, etc.

Getting the first manual underway is the hardest part of the process. Make it a habit for yourself and for your employees to document their daily activities, as this will make it easier to keep your Operations Manuals up to date. I would suggest providing your employees with journals to record their daily work methods, with the stipulation that the journals are company property and will be retained by the company if the employee leaves. Make their journal's part of the employees performance review. This accumulation of information about your business in both formal Operations Manuals and informal journaling will provide deep insight into the operation of your company. Over time you may even discover things about your business that you were not overtly aware of.

Now on to mining the wealth these documents create for you. Obviously a well documented business will fetch a much higher price than a poorly documented business. A well documented business also provides the employees with guidance and direction when the owner is not present, giving the owner the time to spend on more important matters (or even allowing for a well deserved and uninterrupted vacation). But going one step further, a well documented business can actually create new revenue streams for the owner. Every business person is seeking to find and use the "best practices" in their own businesses. A well documented business manual can fetch a handsome price on the open market. Let's suppose you have an outstanding "Customer Service Process" that wins rave reviews from clients, vendors and business partners. Why not sell a copy of your Customer Service Manual to them? You can hire an editor or a ghost writer to "clean up" the manual and a graphic artist can give it a "first class look." You now have a new product to offer not only your immediate client base but the world in general.

The first objection I often hear is "I don't want my competition to know what I'm doing." I'd like you to keep in mind a few things about human nature. People who will buy your information are looking for a solution to a problem. Most want a simple explanation to a complex problem, and unfortunately, complex problems require complex solutions, which is what your information provides. Once the reader begins to understand the complexity, they often choose not to implement. Another interesting fact is that 75% of the people who buy "do it yourself" manuals, eventually hire an expert to do the job for them, which creates still another income stream for you. Plus there will be people who purchase the product and never read it. So the chances are slim that your competitor will not end up using your stuff against you in the long run, And unless you are in a very highly specialized field, there are always enough customers to go around.

Good luck in mining the gold in your business.

George Meidhof is a small business coach, consultant and mentor. His winning combination of experience as a corporate executive and a serial entrepreneur gives George a unique perspective on successful business operation. He has helped numerous entrepreneurs excel in marketing, human resources and financial management, helping them achieve financial and personal freedom. For more information on his services visit www.ConstellationCoaching.com and be sure to sign up for the "Secrets of Success" newsletter.

CHAPTER 41

Your Computer:
The Breath of Your Business

Blue Melnick

As an entrepreneur, I've made the conscious decision to distinguish between smart business and good business. Running a smart business means accepting that my time is finite and my expertise doesn't cover everything, so it's a false economy to try to handle all aspects of my business in-house. Dedicating my time and energy to my core functions—serving my clients and building my business—is smarter than allowing myself to be bogged down with the myriad of other critical tasks.

So, what non-core functions are keeping you from running your business the smart way? I'm willing to bet that the necessary evil of daily offsite computer backup falls into that category.

Dear fellow entrepreneur, I implore you, wake up! In this increasingly digital world, the majority of your income generation takes place on your computer! Whether it's creative work, such as this book, the copy for your marketing pieces, your email communications, or your valuable contact database, your business "lives" on your computer's hard drive. And make no mistake: your computer stores thousands of dollars of information; information that is near impossible to replace once lost.

Consider this question: how much is your digital information actually worth? Using time as the key variable, you can determine a simplified and conservative value of the information being stored on your computer in four simple steps:

1. Estimate the number of hours spent working on your computer each week.
2. Multiply this figure by the hourly rate at which you value your time. This will tell you how much the information on your computer increases in value every week, in simplified terms.
3. Determine the number of weeks that you've conducted business, assuming 48 weeks per year.
4. Now, simply multiply your answer from step 2 by the number of weeks you've been in business (step 3). The result is the simplified and conservative value of your digital information.

Knowing now what your information is worth, I'm sure you'll agree that failing to take full responsibility for the safe keeping of your digital information is a recipe for disaster.

True, you may purchase insurance to help mitigate your losses in the event of disasters such as fires, flooding, theft or sabotage. If one of these scenarios happens, a quick call to your insurance company would start the process of recovering the financial value of your damaged or stolen computer, and you'd likely receive sufficient compensation to purchase a shinny new workhorse. But what about the information stored on your damaged computer? Even if your insurance policy covers information loss (which is extremely unlikely), financial compensation is not going to return your income-generating information. Which begs the next question: what would happen to your business if you were unable to recover or recreate your digital information quickly after a loss?

On a personal note, this happened to me. My hard drive crashed for no apparent reason, but it wasn't the computer that I use for work. It was a computer that stored something of great personal value to me: the only good copy of my wedding video that I had been personally editing together for months.

The bizarre thing was I had just completed editing the video the night before, and I hadn't even had the chance to play it for my wife. All I did was unplug the external drive from my laptop and connect it to my desk top computer, but that was enough to crash the drive, completely erase months of work and destroy all the images of our wedding day.

Though both my wife and I literally felt sick to our stomachs for days afterward, I learned the most important lesson of my career and gained the vision for my life's work. My wife and I co-founded our company with this one undeniable truth: **Your computer backup cannot wait until tomorrow.**

I was lucky, because what if my livelihood had depended on that hard drive? What if it had been my business computer that had crashed? Would my business have survived? I don't believe so, and as I later found out, the statistics concur.

According to the National Archives and Records Administration in Washington, 50% of businesses that lose access to their critical information for 10 days or more file for bankruptcy immediately, and another 43% close their doors within 12 months. Do you see what this means? If you cannot access the information stored on your computer's hard drive for 10 consecutive days, there is a mere 7% chance that your business will survive.

Not convinced? Simply attempt the following experiment: Turn off your computer on Monday morning. Leave it off for the duration of the week, and try to generate income for your business without accessing any of the information on your computer. As you will soon realize, your computer is as important to your business as breath is to your life.

What's more, even if your computer is brand new, your information remains at risk. In February 2007, Google Inc. released a study that they conducted on their own computers entitled *Failure Trends in a Large Disk Drive Population*. According to this study, which was the most extensive of its kind ever completed, hard drives are most likely to fail if they are less than 3 months old or more than 2 years old. Basically, if you think a computer backup is unnecessary because your computer is new, you may be in for a terrible shock.

If at this point in the chapter you have not yet made the decision to protect your digital information utilizing an automatic offsite computer backup, you are instead making the decision to play Russian roulette with your business. I don't want to see you lose that game. So, here are some signs that—if you're lucky enough to notice them—may indicate that your computer is in imminent danger of a crash. I want to emphasize, though, that these warnings may or may not be apparent. The absence of any or all of these signs does not mean that your hard drive is in the clear.

1. Your computer is slow to boot up (turn on)

If you notice that your computer is not starting up quite as quickly as it usually does, and this decrease in speed cannot be attributed to the installation of new anti-virus software, your hard drive may be suffering from bad blocks/sectors.

Your hard drive contains magnetically coated metal disks that spin at a speed of roughly 7200 times per minute. If these disks (or their coating) become damaged in any way, a catastrophic failure is likely within 6 months time.

2. Your computer starts to whir, and/or make noise

A change in the way your computer sounds could indicate that the disks within your hard drive are having difficulty completing their rotation. Remember: your computer has moving parts, and these parts are situated in extremely close proximity to each other. Specks of dust, not visible to the human eye, can damage these disks and impede their movement, let alone the metal fingers that support these disks.

3. Your computer experiences a read/write error, or indicates that a disk has failed to respond

According to the Google Inc. study mentioned above, hard drives are 30 times more likely to fail within 60 days of experiencing an initial scan error, than drives that have yet to receive such errors.

If you are currently backing up your data to CD, tape or external hard drive, you're on the right track, but when was the last time you tested that backup? Moreover, these methods require that you (or your employees) perform the backup and store these unencrypted duplicates in a safe place away from your office. These manual systems tend to break down over time, leaving your information—and your livelihood—in a precarious position.

Alternatively, here's how conscious entrepreneurs can act today to protect their digital information:

1. The absolute best way to protect your computer is not to attempt to protect it against a crash, but to plan for data recovery after a crash. The reason being is there is no fail-safe way to prevent a computer crash.
2. Enlist the services of a reputable IT Service company that offers monthly service contracts, and have them clean and test your hard drive on a regular basis.
3. Ask your computer to scan for errors and bad blocks. Your computer may not be kind enough to automatically alert you when sectors of your hard drive are damaged, but you can ask it to scan for trouble.

As conscious entrepreneurs, we must recognize the value of our digital information, and act responsibly to protect it. Otherwise, we stand to lose everything we've worked so hard to build.

In closing, I ask you to commit, right now, to backing up your computer via a secure offsite storage service. The ability to bounce back quickly from a frightening computer crash is smart business at its best.

Blue Melnick is the co-founder of Virtual Tape Drive Canada: The secure, 100% automated, offsite backup solution that gives you peace-of-mind, and lets you run your business worry-free! Blue is extending a special offer for the readers of this incredible collaboration: simply include the promotional code "Conscious" when contacting us to receive 2 full months of backup service absolutely free. Please visit us online at www.BeCrashReady.com, or call us toll free at 1-866-486-8078.

CHAPTER 42

A Copywriting Crash Course to Reach the Conscious Consumer

Lorrie Morgan-Ferrero

If you're sick and tired of being told the only way to reach your audience is through over-the-top, hype-filled marketing messages that make you want to run from the room screaming, I'm here to tell you there IS another way. It's entirely possible to weave the traditional proven methods of marketing with the **new rising consciousness** of many consumers. There isn't a perfect name that umbrellas all of them, but they're called any of the following:

- Eco-Entrepreneurs
- Cultural Creatives
- LOHAS (Lifestyles of Health and Sustainability)
- Green Businesses
- Conscious Consumers

Whatever you want to call them, they are 62 million strong. That's a pretty tight niche to tap into. As we become more and more aware of how small our planet really is, the more people's values change. Yes, many live in California (like me), but frankly, they are all over the world.

- As far as age goes, in any given year there are slightly fewer conscious consumers in the 18-24 range and the over 70 range.
- They have a wide range of incomes, though mostly on the higher end as

they are well-educated.
- Conscious consumers are actually pretty mainstream in their religious beliefs and affiliations, although there are a few New Agers in the group.
- 60% are women.

Basically they are modern day hippies with money. They are parallel to what politicians refer to as 'women's issues.'
- Empathetic
- Distressed about social wrongs like abuse and violence
- Strong family ties
- Care about relationships

Now one of the things I teach is doing deep target market research. With this group, you HAVE to. They are very unforgiving if you trip up, but very loyal if they buy into your product or service.

In fact, here are some common qualities they all have:
1. Brand loyal
2. Early adopters of innovative ideas
3. Your values are as important to them as theirs are
4. Authenticity is critically important
5. They like to do deep research
6. They are demanding as a demographic

Sales Resistance on the Rise

Have you noticed it? More and more marketing campaigns are going over the top. They're trying bolder, more 'in-your-face' tactics. And consumers DON'T like it.

According to a study by Yankelovich Partners (a marketing company), 60% of consumers have a much more negative opinion of marketing and advertising than they did a few years ago. 65% already feel overwhelmed with too many marketing messages, and 61% feel the volume is out of control. So what do you do?

Beat consumer negativity and resistance by precisely targeting the "tarket" of your audience. Subscribe to the publications they read, both online and offline. Join the groups they're in. Pay attention to how they promote themselves and follow suit.

Once you have a grip on your average target market, you're ready to eliminate all but one. Don't worry. No one gets hurt. It's just for your copy.

You're going to narrow your target market down to a specific **tarket!** The word tarket comes from combining the words "target" plus "market." I coined the term because it's critical you think in the singular, not plural. **Target market sounds like a mob, whereas a tarket is just one person.** Before you do anything...I mean anything, you MUST know how to collect the critical info of who your tarket is. Here is my tarket:

Nikki Stanton, a 37 year old divorced entrepreneur with a web conferencing business. She's Internet and business savvy. Invests most of her profit back into the business. Lives in San Diego in a gated community with her 10 year old daughter, Madison. Involved in daughter's school and drives her to dance classes. Has a home office making approximately $117,000 per year. Jogs 3 times a week in the neighborhood. She loves to find bargains on designer clothes. *And dreams of visiting Italy with her daughter someday.*

(Remember a "tarket" is the single person you write your copy to rather than the mob of your entire "target market". "Target" plus "market" equals "tarket.")

When you tap into the psyche of your tarket, you understand better how to approach your marketing.

The most powerful copy is focused with a clear idea first of the person who is already looking for your product or service. Without doing your research, your message meets resistance every time. Doing your due diligence is cheap insurance against consumer resistance. Know what your tarket wants, not what YOU THINK he or she wants.

Stories Consistently Grab Attention

Once you know who you're marketing to, try using stories to cut through the clutter.

Stories are wickedly effective in getting attention. They work in conversation, and they work like gangbusters in copy. Why?

1. **Stories boost credibility.** In order to tell a good story, you had better know your stuff. When your expertise is illustrated in a story you are more believable.

2. **Stories spark emotional connection.** We buy from an emotional state of mind, not a logical one. And dry facts seldom get us worked into an emotional lather the way stories do.

3. **Stories can explore the pain of a problem.** If you're looking to paint the picture of suffering and agony in order to contrast how you or your service can be the solution, nothing does it better than a juicy story.

4. **Stories make the prospect trust you.** Whenever we hear a story, by nature we look for connections to our own lives (after all, it truly IS all about "me"). That relating slashes the timeframe for bonding. And we all do business with those we know, like and trust.

5. **Stories bust through sales resistance.** Nobody likes to be sold to, but we don't mind kicking back and listening to (or reading) a story. You're much more likely to keep the prospect's attention by telling a story than hitting him or her over the head with hype.

So for your own story inspiration, pay attention to little events that happen to you. Get in the habit of writing them down every day in a notebook you dedicate just to stories. (Type them if you like, but it's been proven there is a connection between writing things out by hand and brain stimulation.) Don't edit at first. Just get it all out there. Over time, you will start getting more concise. The point is to create a habit. It will take a little practice at first, but the payoff is huge.

3 Tragic Mistakes of "Green Marketing"

The growing green market is relatively untapped, but like Marie Antoinette many marketers rush in and lose their heads. While there are many errors committed when trying to reach that sector, these are the three worst mistakes made:

Mistake #1: Dull, boring headlines.

It's hard to keep awake long enough to read the copy in those boring magazines and websites. Headlines like: "Make an impression and you can change the world" "Healthy. Happy. For Real" or "A Natural Partnership"...*yawn.*

Look - The job of the headline is to cut through the clutter and grab your attention. We are exposed to more advertising in one day than our grandparents use to get in an entire year. You've got your work cut out for you if you want to address anybody, and it starts with the headline. Stick with the tried and true attention-grabbing formulas.

Mistake #2: Ignoring long copy.

I know you like to "think" the LOHAS market is just too smart for all that long copy. After all they are made up of wealthy CEOs and soccer moms. Don't be ridiculous. They are a very educated segment of the population which means they make informed decisions. Just like anybody, when it comes down to making a buying decision, LOHAS want all the facts. Long copy continues to prevail because it WORKS. *Now long copy for the sake of being long is plain stupid.* You want copy that overcomes objections, makes a solid case, and answers all the questions in the prospect's mind.

Mistake #3: Not capitalizing on celebrity endorsement.

Ed Begley Jr. is a fixture in Studio City where I live. He has been known to ride his bike to work way before it was cool to look at alternative fuel options. Now he has launched his own environmentally safe cleaning products called *Begley's Best.* Ed's endorsement means something. If you tie a celebrity to a green product, it means instant credibility, so you have a much better chance of succeeding in the LOHAS market.

Remember, you can market to the green folks, using many of the same marketing principles you would use for the regular joe. Come from an authentic position and be respectful. Soon they'll be showing you the green.

Lorrie Morgan-Ferrero of Red Hot Copy.com is among a handful of the most highly sought after copywriters in the information marketing industry, appealing particularly to conscious and female entrepreneurs. To date, Lorrie has helped her clients generate millions of dollars in sales using her rapport-building style of copywriting. A direct descendent of Ralph Waldo Emerson, clients hire Lorrie to write for them or to learn her easy proprietary, step-by-step system for themselves.

CHAPTER 43

Good for Profit—
Your Social Conscience is an Asset
to Your Business

Tracy Lee Needham

It all started with a love of Chocolate Chip Cookie Dough ice cream. I was in college, needing a little extra money, and decided to apply part-time at my favorite scoop shop. It certainly wasn't a glamorous job. By the end of a busy night, my arms would be covered in a rainbow of flavors and I'd be praying for customers to order a cup of something soft like White Russian or Chocolate Raspberry Swirl. Not to mention, I always left smelling like I bathed in a vat of Chunky Monkey®. But it was fun and the customers were always in a good mood—how could you not be when you're eating ice cream?

Unlike most other jobs I've had, I was proud to work there. Yes, I knew plenty of CEO's wrote big checks to charitable causes, but Ben & Jerry's social mission seemed to be encoded into the company's DNA. They didn't just donate money to charity—they involved and educated customers by creating products like Rainforest Crunch and Peace Pops® to benefit causes. They bought the brownie dough from a bakery that employed disadvantaged adults. PartnerShop franchises helped non-profits provide job training to inner-city youth. Even the ice cream waste at their factories was "recycled" by feeding it to pigs on a nearby farm. And of course, they were constantly earning praise for their innovative employment policies and benefits. To me, they were the epitome of what a company could be—making a profit *and* making a difference in the world.

Even now, 20 years later, I will drive past several other ice cream shops for a scoop of Ben & Jerry's. Yes, the ice cream is delicious, but such devoted loyalty is inspired by more than just great ice cream—it's inspired by the desire to support a company you can believe in.

Clients Buy You, Not What You Offer

Scandals like Enron, Tyco, and Qwest Communications have left many Americans looking for companies they can believe in again. It's no longer just a question of "Is this a good deal for me?", but also "Is this a good company to buy from?" Furthermore, the standards bar for what makes a "good company" continues to rise. In fact, a recent survey showed that 83% of Americans believe companies should support charitable causes and 93% said they have a responsibility to help preserve the environment.

As a result, many corporate giants are finally waking up to the fact that "social profit" is as valuable an objective as financial profit. According to Leonard Berry in *Discovering the Soul of Service*, a company creates social profit by sharing its talents, leadership, and money to make a bigger, more meaningful difference in the world around them.

Research shows that social profit boosts the bottom line because it enhances your company's reputation and visibility, converts customers into loyal fans, and enriches employee recruitment and retention. As for its impact on sales, consider this: more than two-thirds of Americans say they consider a company's business practices, such as its environmental friendliness and treatment of employees, when deciding what to buy. And 87% of consumers will choose a company that supports a worthy cause over one that doesn't, if price and quality are similar. So the extra "feel good" factor can actually be a pretty powerful incentive.

Social Profit Benefits All Businesses, Large and Small

Corporate giants are spending billions of dollars today on initiatives designed to make them appear more socially and environmentally conscious. Yet many conscious solopreneurs and small business owners are already pursuing the same kinds of initiatives—just on a smaller and less formalized scale. We give money, volunteer our time, recycle, and try to become more energy efficient because it's the right thing to do. We look for ways to recruit and retain valued employees because it's just common sense that happy employees will translate into happier, more profitable customers.

Unfortunately, we're leaving a lot of potential value on the table when we overlook these efforts or dismiss them as irrelevant to our "real business"—especially those of us in service industries. Think about it. We are essentially marketing a promise that we will do what we say and provide what the client needs on time, on budget, and on the mark. Often, we ask them to start paying for those services before they see what they'll actually receive. And of course, we know there are plenty of competitors lurking nearby who say they can provide similar services, sometimes for less. Ultimately, the potential client's decision isn't about the services themselves, but about whom she likes and trusts more. Your social and environmental initiatives give her insight into your values and help establish that all-important emotional connection.

The good news for conscious solopreneurs and small businesses is that *quality* and *effectiveness* of your efforts matter more than quantity. Creating a strategic plan for your social profit initiatives is the best way to achieve that. By setting a budget, establishing goals, mapping out the path, communicating your efforts, and measuring your results – you can leverage your limited resources for maximum impact.

Tips for creating your Social Profit Plan:

1. Focus, focus, focus. Instead of haphazardly writing a lot of small checks and volunteering here and there, choose one cause to rally behind. Ideally it should be one you are enthusiastic about, that is relevant to your company's mission, and which appeals to your target market.

The same goes for environmental initiatives. Choose one or two areas that are relevant to your business instead of trying to tackle everything at once. Reducing waste and energy efficiency are usually good places to start.

Keep in mind that the cause or initiative itself is not nearly as important as having a genuine commitment to it. Customers are becoming increasingly savvy at distinguishing genuine efforts from purely promotional ones.

2. Identify where you can have the largest impact. For your charitable efforts, look for one organization which represents your cause and allows you to be a visible, big fish in a small pool. It's far better to support a number of events and projects throughout the year than to be one sponsor among many for a single big event. Consider how you can leverage resources besides cash as well. Who could most use your expertise, your excess equipment, your office space? How could you involve your customers? Also, be sure to consult your accountant about what types of donations you will and won't be able to deduct from the company's taxes.

Environmentally, look for opportunities that can save you money in the long run, such as replacing incandescent lighting with fluorescent and halogen bulbs, or exchanging outdated equipment for new Energy Star models. Also, where's the easiest place to start so you can get the momentum going?

3. Get the word out. Send out press releases. Post articles and photos on your web site and in your newsletter. Hang signs in your office that explain what you're doing. Instead of a "look how great we are" message, talk about why you're doing this and share stories that show how the non-profit is benefiting.

Make the results of your efforts to go green visual. Again, photos can help, or go online to find equivalents that paint a picture. It's much easier for people to relate to statements such as "The newspapers we recycled would form a stack 12 feet high" or "The energy we saved could power 200 homes for a year!" than citing pounds or kilowatts reductions. Applying for small-business oriented green designations such as Co-op America's Business Seal of Approval, and Energy Star's Small Business Program can help as well.

4. Measure and evaluate the results. Whatever initiatives you choose, you must track your progress and results to see what's effective and worthwhile—for both you and your non-profit partner. It'll also provide valuable material for your communications.

Far from being irrelevant, your social conscience is an *asset* to your business. It can differentiate you from competitors, forge stronger connections with prospects and clients, and enhance public perception about your company. All of which translates into a stronger, more sustainable business. It can also create a company to believe in -- one that really does make a difference in the world.

Tracy Needham, founder of Compelling Communications, LLC, aims to make marketing less painful and more effective for solopreneurs and small businesses. Sign up for her FREE Report The One Press Release You Can Write to Get Thousands of Dollars Worth of Free Publicity at www.compellingcomm.com and you'll also get FREE Compelling Marketing ezine— full of insider secrets and resources to help you attract more clients and make more money while maximizing your time and budget.

CHAPTER 44

How a 100-Year Business Plan Will Make You Rich!

Alexis Martin Neely

As a creative, conscious entrepreneur myself, I am intimately aware of my own desire to live in the moment, focus on the now, and not project into the future. While these spiritual principles guide my day to life and keep me sane as my business grows, my long-term business success requires them to be grounded in a long-term vision for my business and for my life.

If you are serious about building a business that will have a lasting impact on your family, your customers, and our planet as a whole, you've got to ask yourself some questions that have no easy answers. But if you ask these questions at the very beginning of your business venture (or as soon as you can if your business is already under way), the answers will guide you to build a business that is not only authentically you, but is primed to make a real difference in the world.

The first and most important question to ask yourself is **what is your exit strategy from your business?** You've heard Stephen Covey tell you to "Begin with the end in mind" if you want to be personally successful. Well, it's exactly the same for your business. You've got to be clear about what you want to happen to your business after you are ready to move on.

Here are some scenarios to consider. Would you like to sell your business 5 years from now? If so, for how much? Do you want to retire from your business 20 years from now? Or, do you see your business as something you will hand down to family members who will run it while you continue to pull in passive income? Are you creating a business that will be here 100 years from now, and if so, what will it look like then?

Before moving on to read the rest of this chapter, **spend a few minutes now writing down your exit strategy for your business.**

Next, **ask yourself what your business would look like 3 or 5 years from now if it were an absolute and total success and you knew without a shadow of a doubt you could not fail.**

If you are like most people, you are not thinking as big about your business as you possibly can, which means that you are not serving as many people as you possibly could and not making a big enough impact on the world. What does your business look like when it's successful beyond your wildest dreams? How many people are you serving when your business is as triumphant as you can imagine? How is it serving? How is it making the world a better place?

Using your answers to these questions as a guide, **write down the ultimate success vision for your business now.** If you begin to feel a bit queasy or foggy as you do this, push through it. That's fear. On the other side is a glorious sight. Just start writing something - anything. It can change and grow as you do, but you've got to get it down to get it started.

Third, **ask yourself how much money you want to be making from your business in 1, 3 and 5 years from today, and if you were going to sell your business down the road what your sale number will be.**

Write down all of these numbers and post them where you can see them everyday. Each morning when you sit down at your desk, look at these numbers and know without a doubt you will get there. It helps me to remember the story of funny man, actor Jim Carrey, who in 1985 with only $10,000 in the bank, wrote himself a check for $10,000,000 and dated it for Thanksgiving of 1995 and noted in the memo "For acting services rendered." As the story goes, just before Thanksgiving of 1995, Jim found out he'd be paid $10,000,000 for the movie Dumb and Dumber.

Don't be afraid to think big. You can achieve what you believe is possible. Of course, the key is believing it's possible. Don't write down money goals that you don't believe are possible. If you are a teacher, it's unlikely you are going to receive a check for $10,000,000 for teaching, but if you build a national tutoring business, it is entirely reasonable that you could sell it one day for $10,000,000.

Whatever you do, **don't get trapped in the belief that being a conscious entrepreneur means you can't make bushels of money.** You can make boatloads of money and be conscious at the same time.

As Wayne Dyer says, "Successful people make money. It's not that people who make money become successful, but that successful people attract money. They bring success to what they do."

Now that you've got your exit strategy, the ultimate success vision for your business, and your money goals, you can stop projecting into the future and focus on the now of your business, which means **setting your business up right from the beginning in such a way that you are showing the Universe you mean business about your business success.**

To do that, you will first want to **establish your business using the right corporate form** to allow you to take maximum business risk with minimum personal exposure.

A sole proprietorship/DBA is not the way to go. I don't care how conscious you are, s**t happens that could mean personal liability for you. And, if you are serious about growing your business, you've got to establish a corporate shield to show the Universe you are serious about that growth.

There are many different options for this, including a Limited Liability Company (LLC), a C-Corporation, or an S-Corporation. The type of entity you choose is not a decision to be made lightly, nor is it a decision to be made without the guidance of a trusted advisor who knows your personal situation.

The work that you've done up until now identifying your exit strategy, your ultimate success vision and your money goals should be shared with your legal advisor and your tax advisor. These advisors will guide you to the right decision about the kind of entity you should use for your business.

Establishing these relationships early in your business will allow you to focus your creative genius on what Strategic Coach Dan Sullivan calls your Unique Ability®. Unless the study of complex legal, tax and financial issues is your Unique Ability, you've got to have a team in place to guide your decisions about these issues for the long-term success of your company.

Don't fall into the trap of believing you can just go on the internet and get the form documents and answers you need. I've seen far too many business owners make that mistake and live to regret it. In fact, I was one myself. Here's just one example.

I figured as a smart person and a lawyer, I could establish my own financial record keeping systems for my business. Big mistake! This was an ego-based decision, not one made with conscious awareness of my own Unique Ability®, which is definitely not bookkeeping.

Over the first two years of my business, I proceeded to mess up my books so seriously that it cost me tens of thousands of dollars to repair the damage I had done. My desire to save money actually cost me a whole lot more in the long run.

Had I been acting truly consciously, I would have been aware of my Unique Ability®, trusted that all of the resources I would need would be there, and I would have made the investment to find the best possible professionals to set things up and maintain them for me in the right way, which would return my investment many times over.

Surround yourself with a knowledgeable professional team including a lawyer, a banker and an accountant/tax person and you will have the team you need to fulfill your 100-year vision.

The kind of professional you want on your team in any of these areas is someone who asks what your long-range vision is for your business before recommending any strategies. There are plenty of people out there who can provide 'one size fits all' products and form documents, but you are looking for advisors who will develop solutions that are customized to your vision and your goals, and meet with you strategically every year to update your vision and your planning. With this clear vision in mind of what you want, you'll find them.

Last, but not least, you will want to get totally self aware about two things: 1) your Unique Ability®, what I call your Creative Genius - that one thing that comes so easily to you that you love doing so much, and that provides so much value in the world that it's clear you shouldn't be doing anything but that and 2) your Energy Suckers - those things that you can do and continue to do because they seem easy for you, but you don't love doing them and you aren't that great at them. Then, you can focus on doing as much of your Creative Genius as possible and find the best team you can possibly have to take care of your Energy Suckers. That takes true self-awareness, and self-awareness is what being a conscious entrepreneur is all about.

Alexis Martin Neely is the Personal Family Lawyer you love. As a mom, writer, speaker and entrepreneur herself, Alexis knows how hard it can be to stay awake and aware while dealing with the day to day of building a business, raising children and paying the bills. Get Alexis' $49 audio CD "Show the Universe You Mean Business About Your Business" free at www. FamilyWealthMatters.com/business, or contact the Family Wealth Planning Institute at 866-999-3974. Use Code CE08.

CHAPTER 45

10 Strategies for Turning Your Dreams into a Profitable Business

Roxanne Pennington

Have you ever dreamed of turning your passion into a profitable business? Growing up in Kansas, I couldn't have been much farther from the ocean. Now I live on the beach in Florida, travel the world, and swim with humpback whales, wild dolphins, whale sharks, and sea turtles. Most importantly, I have built a successful business doing exactly what I love. DiveTravel.com is an international portal of all scuba related businesses and dive travel destinations. We provide articles, resources and links for scuba divers and ocean lovers. Here are ten strategies to help you experience success as a conscious entrepreneur.

1. Discover your Passion

"Make no little plans; they have no magic to stir men's blood...Make big plans, aim high in hope and work."

~ DANIEL H. BURNHAM

What are your passions, interests and hobbies? What lights you up and doesn't seem like work at all? Is there a childhood passion that can be rekindled? I have always loved the water, photography, and traveling. My husband, David and I are avid scuba divers and dreamed of starting a business together leading dive trips. So when my Professor of Entrepreneurship, Dr. Gary Roberts asked me to create a business plan, I decided to incorporate these passions into a specialty travel agency for scuba diving expeditions. When Dr. Roberts read my plan he said, "You *have* to do this!" His words of encouragement motivated me to take a leap of faith, resign from my job, and launch DiveTravel.com in September 2002.

2. Plan for Success

"A goal without a plan is just a wish."

~ ANTOINE DE SAINT EXUPÉRY (1900-1944)

Set goals to accomplish your dreams and stretch beyond your comfort zone. Start with the end in mind when creating your plan. My goal in college was to get a 4.0 so I found out what each professor required for an "A." I created a plan and recorded important dates and milestones that I needed to reach along the way. I still use this method today in business. I look for areas where people are having problems and create a game plan for developing a product or service that provides a solution. Conscious entrepreneurs plan for success by focusing on the end result and mapping out a plan to achieve their goals.

3. Take Risks! Feel the Fear and Do it Anyway.

"One doesn't discover new lands without consenting to lose sight of the shore for a very long time."

~ ANDRÉ GIDE

Step out in faith and take action to achieve your goals. Although I love to swim, I was a bit anxious about learning to scuba dive. I was afraid that I'd feel claustrophobic. From the first night of class when I breathed from a regulator, I was hooked. It was completely relaxing to lie at the bottom of the pool with no sound except for that of my own breathing. I love looking up and seeing the sunlight as it hits the water. Thankfully, I overcame my fears and learned to scuba dive.

4. Monitor and Adjust

"A good plan, violently executed now, is better than a perfect plan next week."

~ GEORGE S. PATTON

When you launch a business, there are hypothetical numbers involved in the forecast. You create a business plan knowing that it can be modified later. At DiveTravel.com we revised our business model. Operating a specialty travel agency for scuba divers and leading expeditions was a high risk, labor-intensive venture with a low profit margin. We transitioned to an information marketing model that made money, even while we slept. Now we can provide more information to more customers. Instead of being a small travel company, we are now using the full power of the DiveTravel.com domain to bring divers together with all the scuba diving businesses.

5. Strive for Excellence

"The quality of a person's life is in direct proportion to their commitment to excellence, regardless of their chosen field of endeavor."

~ VINCENT T. LOMBARDI

Operate with integrity and strive for excellence in everything you do. Show up, on time, dressed and ready to play. Athletes at the top of their game continue to practice and improve their skills. In business, excellence is reflected in every e-mail, every conversation; everything you say and do. We strive for excellence in communication by being clear, direct, and honest. We look for opportunities to exceed our customers' expectations because they are like oxygen to the body and the reason the business continues to thrive. We look for employees and vendors with the same philosophy of excellence.

6. Have Laser Focus

"I'm a great believer in luck, and I find the harder I work the more I have of it."

~ Thomas Jefferson

Be intentional with your actions. Don't allow distractions to steal your time and energy. When I was working full time at WORLDSPAN and going to college full time, I *had* to focus. My time was so limited that I often thought, "OK, what has to happen in the next 10 minutes?" For me, watching movies and TV had to go. What tempts you and wastes your time? Time is a vacuum the world will fill up if you are not intentional with your actions. We each have 24 hours in a day, so it is what we do with our time that makes the difference.

7. Learn and Implement

"The great aim of education is not knowledge but action."

~ Herbert Spencer

Learning is half the equation; the other half is taking action and implementing the ideas. As the daughter of two teachers, the importance of education was instilled in me at an early age. I was taught that I could be anything I wanted to be if I studied hard and made good grades. I still look for opportunities to expand my knowledge. That is why continuing education is a core value of our business and we spend thousands of dollars each year on books, training programs, home study courses, attending conferences, seminars, and webinars.

8. Build a Team

"To succeed as a team is to hold all of the members accountable for their expertise."

~ Mitchell Caplan, CEO, E*Trade Group Inc.

As an entrepreneur, your role is to create a business by getting specialized knowledge and implement a system. Once the system is in place, hire high-caliber employees to operate your business. If I had it to do over again, I wouldn't have waited to hire a team. I waited until there was "extra" money for salaries. If you fall into this trap, I encourage you to calculate the number of sales you need to cover the additional expense of salaries. Once I did have my team in place, I was able to focus on the activities that only I could do. I felt a freedom and peace of mind knowing experts in their field were handling daily operations, even when I was out of the office. A team creates good energy and synergy, so goals are quickly achieved.

9. Find a Mentor and Mastermind Group
"As iron sharpens iron, so one man sharpens another."

PROVERBS 27:17

Just as professional athletes have coaches, mentors are business coaches that work with you to improve your skills and evaluate every area of your business. You can benefit at every stage from working with a mentor to keep you at the top of your game. My mentors have taught me their secrets to creating wealth, managing time, people, and activities while remaining organized and focused. My International Mastermind group is a team of highly educated, professional, and goal-oriented individuals. We teleconference monthly and meet quarterly to focus and critique our businesses, brainstorm on current challenges, and work to perfect our marketing skills. My mentors and Mastermind group have played a key role in my success.

10. Make a Difference
"We make a living by what we get, we make a life by what we give."
~ SIR WINSTON CHURCHILL

What will be your legacy? Your life on Earth is but a moment in eternity so make a difference while you are here. Contribute time and money to organizations you believe in. My goal is to educate people about the ocean. Did you know that the ocean covers over 70 percent of the Earth's surface?

It is at risk due to pollution, over fishing, and rising temperatures. Without coral, the amount of carbon dioxide in the water rises and that affects *every living thing* on Earth. I encourage you to be a global thinker and get involved in causes that inspire you.

Conclusion

If you are not living an abundant life, create a plan and take action to alter the trajectory of your life. I have successfully combined my passions for scuba diving, photography and world travel into a profitable business. I am blessed and having the best time of my life. It is possible to have a career and a life that you are passionate about and the rewards are well worth it. Make a difference and create a life you love!

Successful entrepreneur, published author, speaker, and ocean advocate, Roxanne Pennington is the founder and CEO of several companies including DiveTravel.com. Roxanne's books, articles, and training programs encompass Business, Personal Finance and Investing, Aquatic Sports, Adventure Travel, Group Expeditions, Photography, Videography, and Oceanography. Roxanne is a Certified Travel Counselor (CTC) and earned a Bachelors Degree in Finance and MBA from Kennesaw State University, Georgia. For your FREE copy of "Selling with Integrity", go to www.Conscious-Selling.com.

CHAPTER 46

The Conscious Entrepreneur's Blueprint to Earn Passive Revenue with Information Products

James Roche

Yes, you can be spiritual AND make plenty of money at the same time. In fact, the secret to wealth is already within you. I believe you have a special spark inside that allows you to solve specific problems in your own unique way. And the beautiful part is…people will pay you to solve their problems with your special, core gift.

Imagine a way to positively impact the greatest number of people with your core gift. Imagine the tens of thousands of lives you can help…if you can only reach them. This "dream" is a reality for a select few conscious entrepreneurs who package and sell their knowledge into information products: books, eBooks (electronic books), audio CD's, teleclasses, special reports, workbooks, live workshops, coaching programs, and many more.

The big mistake I see most conscious entrepreneurs make when they try to create info products is diving right into the content without first creating a strategy to create and marketing their info product. I will show you how to avoid this massive mistake so you create an info product that fully expresses your gift to the world while making you rich!

It starts by uncovering that unique spark within you.

Your Core Gift

Your core gift is the theme of your life expressed in all the things you do and love in life. Who you are – your unique strengths – are integral to the heart of your business. Look back over your life and you'll see your core gift expressed everywhere. It's in the games you played as a kid, in your past careers, and in your education path. And it's probably why you chose to be a conscious entrepreneur.

Even countries have core gifts – it's what they believe in as a core value, what they are known for. What do you think is the core value of America? Freedom! When you think of Germany, what do you think of? Order! How about Italy? Family! It's the same in the arts – although you may not be able to put a word to it. Look at The Beatles. Their sound was so unique, it's instantly recognizable. When you see a Picasso, you know it's a Picasso.

You and your business are no different. What's the core theme of your business? How do you bring your core gift to the people you serve? Your info products will come out of your core gift. This will help you distinguish your products and business from everybody else's.

A Simple Exercise That Can Change Your Business Forever

This may sound simple, but it's key to your success with info products - identify what your business is really about. Because many conscious entrepreneurs are borderline ADD, it's important to hone in on one topic and create your products around that.

Here's a simple exercise to find your topic that I think you'll find very enlightening...

Imagine stepping into your local bookstore. Push open the door and feel that rush of cool air. Smell that new-book smell. Somewhere in this bookstore is your book. Think of your book as the embodiment of your business – it represents what your business is all about. (If you already have a book, still play along to make sure your business is on track.)

Stand in the bookstore and notice the signs hanging from the ceiling with general topics: fiction, history, self-help, etc. In your minds eye, start to walk towards the topic your book is under.

Standing under the sign of your general topic, look at the bookcases. Notice the sub-topics listed on the shelves. For example, under business you may find leadership, management, investing, etc. (To give you an idea, my sub-topic is marketing.)

Go to the shelf with your sub-topic.

Now imagine looking for your last name among the books and pick out your book. Remember, your book represents what your whole business is about so feel yourself pulling out your book. Look at the cover. What's the subject of the book?

For example, in my business I go to the "Business" section first. My sub-topic is "Marketing" and as I pull out my book, I see it's about "Info Products."

You can do this exercise in real life. Go to your local bookstore this week and try it out. If you get stuck, go to the information counter and ask an assistant to show you books about ____ (Fill in the blank with general information about what you do.)

(As a side note, it's really fun to see who your neighbors will be on the book shelves. Look up your last name and see who you're next to.)

The Secret to Passive Revenue with Info Products

There's a secret art to making money with your business topic…and that is **not** selling your topic. What people buy isn't the tangible thing you sell – they buy the core benefit of what you sell. You buy a drill bit because you want a hole, not because you want another piece of metal around the house. You buy eyeglasses because you want clearer vision.

Imagine if you had to sell wall paint. Most people would talk about colors and price, but not you! As a savvy conscious entrepreneur you can tune into the bigger picture – you don't sell paint, you sell happy walls!

Before creating your info product, get clear on what you're really selling. People don't buy information for information's sake alone. It's the bigger benefit people are buying – an end result.

Find the Niche That Makes You Rich

You may have been told you need a niche...and it's frustrating to discover your particular gift. Most conscious entrepreneurs are good at tons of things – it's hard to narrow down all your talents and passions to one thing. And everyone needs what you offer, right?

Well...

There's a HUGE difference between what you **think** people need and what they **actually want**. No matter how passionate you feel about your subject, people only pull out their wallets for what they want. I personally love opera (It's crazy – I know. I grew up listening to my Mom and Dad play Elvis and my brother play Led Zeppelin.) I think you should really, really go see an opera. There's nothing else like it. In fact, go spend $200 to see an opera by Wagner. Sure they're 5 hours long...but you'll love it! You must go!

Convinced?

If you have no interest in spending money on opera, there's no amount of "selling" I can do to change your mind. That's why you only want to find people who are hungry for what you offer. "Everybody" is NOT your target market!

Here's a simple technique to find your target market...

On a fresh piece of paper create two columns. In the left column list all the problems you solve with your Core Gift and business. In the right column list all the groups of people who need those problems solved.

Choose a group that looks like an obvious choice – they have a clear problem and they want what you offer.

Choose the Topic of Your Info Product

You now have all the important elements to create a winning info product: your core gift, your topic, and a target market. The next step is easy...choosing the topic of your info product.

You can make your life very easy or very hard here. The easy path is to simply ask your target market what they want most and give it to them. The hard path is to try to figure this out on your own.

Let your target guide you. Ask them what their single greatest challenge is around your topic. Another great way to identify what products to create is notice what people complain about the most. For example, if you teach sales, you may hear people complain that they don't know to separate themselves from their competition. Simply take what they say and add "How to" in front – that's your info product! For example, "How to Separate Yourself from the Competition for Greater Sales."

Create Your Info Product

You're now ready to produce your info product. This is also easy to do. Remember: you want to leverage your information, so one way to start is give a teleclass on your product topic. Record it, transcribe it and package it with some nice graphics. You're ready to make money with your knowledge!

Info products are one of the simplest and best ways for the conscious entrepreneur to make money doing what they love. You already have the expertise hidden in your Core Gift – you've had it all your life. You now have the opportunity to share your gift with the world and fulfill one of your life's purposes.

James Roche, "The Info Product Guy," helps conscious entrepreneurs get more clients and make passive revenue with info products. He is the creator of the Info Marketing Action Plan (iMap), which shows you step-by-step how to build wealth and info products. To learn more about his simple, step-by-step programs and receive a free Special Report, go to www.InfoProductGuy.com.

CHAPTER 47

If You Build It... *Will They Come?*

Conscious Marketers Sell Dreams

Joy Schechter

In the movie, *Field of Dreams*, a quiet voice from the great beyond whispers to us, "If you build it, [they] will come." In business, that is not exactly true. Sure, you may build it, but if prospects don't know you exist or where to find you, they won't come. And worse, they *won't buy!* How long can anyone stay in business without customers? Or, without repeat customers?

Becoming a 'Conscious Entrepreneur' is the first step to having a life and business filled with purpose, passion and prosperity. If you are new to being a 'Conscious Entrepreneur', at times you will feel a tug of war between the need to make money, the desire to make a difference, and a cry from the depths of your soul to be true to yourself, your dream, your vision. As a 'Conscious Entrepreneur' myself, the only way I have found to be in harmony with all these desires is through Marketing.

"Marketing?" you may ask. Yes, Marketing. It's all about being visible, credible and respected in your field. Marketing is also the process by which you communicate what you have to offer to your customers. "That's all well and good", you might say, "but I need to make money to stay in business." And you're absolutely right... except when you focus on the money without Marketing.

Money Mindset = Mayhem

When you focus exclusively on money, that's all there is (round and round; money in, money out) with no end in sight. Said another way, what you focus on is what you get. It's like constantly running on a treadmill of "Where is the money going to come from?" and having to scramble for your next client or product.

The misconception is this: if we only had the money, then we would have the freedom to take the actions we need to in our business and *then* have the life we want. "Ahhh, peace at last. It's all handled"... or so we think. Instead, it just causes chaos and mischief, like the tail wagging the dog, where the money (or lack of it) drives the business instead of having your passion and dreams be in the driver's seat.

Unfortunately, I've worked with numerous clients whose sole focus was on the money and how to keep it from disappearing. They would create systems and processes to build a better cash/money machine. But operating a cash machine is *not* the same as operating a business. All it did for them was to maintain their struggling and suffering on a non-stop treadmill. However, by introducing Marketing into the equation, it allowed them to run a simpler and more profitable business.

Marketing Mindset = Money (Profitability)

The solution is to take what you are passionate about, at the heart of your inspiration, and market that. It wasn't until Kevin Costner's character, Ray Kinsella, allowed what he was passionate about to come *alive*, that he was able to market his dream. When Terrance Mann (James Earl Jones) gets to know Ray and his dream, he's able to trust him and join the enterprise.

Being visible and credible are core elements to Marketing. You have to *choose* to be visible and it takes *courage* to put yourself out there. Becoming visible is *not* about you personally (with all your flaws and imperfections). Rather, becoming visible is about having the larger picture of the dream being front and center. And dreams attract each other, but only when they are visible, can they find each other. If you can't see it (the dream), you can't move and manage it. By extension, if your customers can't see you – they can't buy from you.

Now that they have found you, they need to know you are credible; that you know your stuff. For instance, a higher degree or certification says someone has taken the time and steps to learn their field, or has X number of years of experience. Without having some sort of credentials, credibility can be earned or confirmed by being professional, reliable, recognized by your peers, and such.

Build a Comfort Zone

In the movie, the second time Ray hears the voice, it tells him to "ease his pain." Every client has a problem or obstacle that is in the way of his or her success. If you can serve your client to help them figure out what the roadblock is *and* to see a way to remove it, it is a win for them and for you. They are thankful to be problem free and you have created a fan for life.

Next, it will take a step beyond Marketing to actually get them to *buy* your service of clearing the roadblocks. Visibility and credibility *plus* being of service to your customers will allow them to feel comfortable, at home with you, and only then are they willing to buy from you. I call this the *comfort zone*. Test it out. Try to sell something to a customer *before* they are in the *comfort zone* and see how hard it is. Would you spend thousands of dollars for a product from a company you didn't know, like or trust? People don't buy products; they buy the *idea* of what the product will provide for them. *Your* product provides *their* freedom from the problems and the pain.

Sell Without Selling

The best sales people I know are *Marketing Masters*. They create that *comfort zone*, extend an invitation (ask for the order) and authentically let you choose for yourself. Too often selling has come to mean you are trying to convince, entice or flat out manipulate people into buying your product.

I've heard it said, "Everyone wants to buy, but no one wants to be sold." This type of selling usually comes about because the product is not in alignment with the customer's needs or wants. Personally, I don't like being sold to. It just gives me the willies and it feels like the presenter is either not skilled or simply doesn't respect my ability to choose.

Consider our discussion earlier about the cash machine. Do you only want them to buy in the moment (make that sale - feed the machine) or do you want to create customers for life? I'm often reminded that it's much easier to keep a current client than to create a new one. A stable of adoring fans beats out struggling to find new clients any day.

Workshops <u>Are</u> Marketing Tools

One of the best vehicles I've found for Marketing and creating the *comfort zone* are **Workshops** (or Seminars, Teleclasses and the like). You have an attentive audience for hours (or days) where they get to know you and trust you. With that accomplished, you deliver your invaluable content and invite them to consider what's next. With this process, sales occur as seamless and can be quite lucrative inside this arena.

Workshops, however, are *not* innately money makers in themselves. The biggest obstacle to their success is that speakers think that the *sole purpose* of the workshop is to make money. They often think the workshop IS the product, *or* that the products sold at the workshop are the reason for holding the workshop in the first place. It is a common trap that perpetuates the cash machine mayhem over and over again.

Some events are designed as cash machines, but that is rare and the majority not only loses a lot of money, but loses the esteem of the people attending. Sure, given that there are people in the room, someone is bound to buy; however, *will they value the experience <u>and</u> tell their friends about it?*

That's why workshops are the perfect vehicle for Marketing. The most successful workshops I've produced are where the participants walk out glowing and exclaim how much they are getting out of the experience; how confident and comfortable they feel with the material. It's even better when the speaker feels the same way. I know in that moment, that the *'zone'* (of comfort) was created and the sales will follow. Happy participants want more and are willing to pay for it. *Even if they don't buy in the moment, you will have created adoring fans for life.* And either way, the event becomes a profitable one.

Putting It All Together

Finally, the voice encourages Ray to "go the distance" and we see him do whatever it takes to fulfill his dream. Likewise, to truly be successful in business means having the courage to do whatever it takes to be true to your vision *and* to be at the forefront of guiding it. Choices like becoming a Marketing Master, serving your customers, applying strategies and tactics (like workshops and the *comfort zone*) are all part of being a 'Conscious Entrepreneur.' And that's just the beginning of the magic.

As Terrance Mann asserts, "If [you] have the courage to go through with this, what a story it will make." Now get to work on building the business of your dreams, so *when you build it, they will come.*

Joy Schechter, Event Strategies and Management Consultant, helps entrepreneurs develop workshops and seminars to successfully market their businesses. Joy combines 25+ years experience in seminar management, event planning, business, corporate and film industries to bring a totally fresh perspective on how to incorporate practical business tools and strategies for increasing profits and client retention. To attend upcoming courses or receive your **FREE** report: 11 Costly Workshop Mistakes and Improving Profitability please visit www.WorkshopSeminarSuccess.com/cebook or email her Joy@WorkshopSeminarSuccess.com.

Free Resources
How to Avoid the Three Massive Mistakes Made by Most Conscious Entrepreneurs!

If you consider yourself a conscious entrepreneur and want to learn how to avoid the pitfalls along the journey and experience success, you'll want to download this FREE special report. It's part of the Conscious Business Success Kit at **www.LoveYourLife.com**

Conscious Business Connection Newsletter

Interested in learning valuable tips, tools, inspiration and strategies for your soulful success? Conscious Business Connection is Christine Kloser's FREE newsletter delivered every other Tuesday via email. Visit **www.LoveYourLife.com** to start your complimentary subscription as part of your FREE Conscious Business Success Kit.

How to Quickly and Easily Grow Your Business... as an Author

Do you have dreams of writing a book to grow your business and share your transformational message with the world? Most conscious entrepreneurs do. But, knowing how to get your book done can be very tricky (the industry sadly has some "unconscious" entrepreneurs). Download this audio as part of Christine Kloser's FREE Conscious Business Success Kit to take your first step toward publishing success. Visit **www.LoveYourLife.com** and enter your name and email on the right side of the homepage.

An Invitation from Christine

FREE 30-Day membership in my Conscious Business Circle

"I believe that continual learning and implementing are critical elements to your success as a Conscious Entrepreneur. That's why I'm inviting you to learn from me FREE for 30 days in my Conscious Business Circle!"
~Christine Kloser

The Conscious Business Circle is your **one-stop resource to get everything you need** to enjoy a purpose-driven, profitable business and a soul-satisfying life!

The Conscious Business Circle connects conscious entrepreneurs with **tips, tools, strategies,** resources and inspiration to **manifest** a mega-successful, conscious business.... with more **ease, grace and joy!!** This exclusive membership program is guaranteed to help you **focus** on your priorities, **connect** to your big vision, create your action plan, and stay on the **cutting-edge** of business and success strategies... consciously!

Get your FREE 30-Day membership now!
www.ConsciousBusinessCircle.com

I look forward to seeing you in "the circle."

Christine

Christine Kloser
Compiler/Publisher, *Conscious Entrepreneurs*
Author, *The Freedom Formula*

Do You Have A Book Inside You?

Most entrepreneurs do. Becoming a published author is, by far, the single most effective tool available to market your business and gain instant credibility, visibility and profitability. But, publishing a book on your own can be an expensive, confusing and exhausting journey.

This is why Love Your Life Publishing was established. We help entrepreneurs like you become published authors quickly, easily and affordably… without the headache and heartache so many aspiring authors experience. If you feel called to share your story, ideas, wisdom, message, process, etc. on the pages of a book, perhaps Love Your Life can help!

Simply visit **www.LoveYourLife.com/products** to learn more about our publishing services. We have three fantastic programs to help turn your publishing dreams into reality.

While you're at the site, be sure to pick up my audio program, *7 Strategies Entrepreneurial Authors Need to Know Before Writing a Word* which is part of my FREE Conscious Business Success Kit. Once you're at the site, simply enter your name and email address in the top right corner of the page to receive your audio instantly.

About Christine Kloser

Christine Kloser is the President of Love Your Life LLC, an inspirational business coach, engaging speaker, and the compiler/publisher of *Conscious Entrepreneurs: A Radical New Approach to Purpose, Passion and Profit*. She has also authored *The Freedom Formula: How to Put Soul in Your Business and Money in Your Bank*; and the *Inspiration to Realization* book series. Christine has been an entrepreneur since 1991; continually exploring new ways to integrate her spiritual understandings with strategic business tactics for herself and her clients. She provides lectures, training, book publishing services and coaching to thousands of entrepreneurs worldwide.

Christine has been nationally recognized as a business and empowerment expert. In addition to her own books, her business and success advice has been featured in the books: *The Ugly Truth about Small Business* by Ruth King, *Web Wonder Women* by Lynne Klippel, *What No One Ever Tells You About Starting Your Own Business* by Jan Norman, *Empowering Women to Power Network* by Ponn M. Sabra, *Heart of a Woman* by Sheryl Rousch and the New York Time Bestseller *Secrets of the Millionaire Mind* by T. Harv Eker. A former television host, columnist and seasoned interviewer, Christine has appeared on numerous radio and television programs and has been featured in **Entrepreneur Magazine**, the **Los Angeles Times, The Portland Press** and **Woman's Day**. Her insights and articles are regularly published in her FREE *Conscious Business Connection* ezine.

Christine Kloser

Love Your Life, LLC

PO Box 2, Dallastown, PA 17313

Ph: (800) 930-3713

www.LoveYourLife.com

For quantity discounts, promotions or sponsorship of Conscious Entrepreneurs, *please call (800) 930-3713 ext. 1.*